INDIGENOUS PEOPLE'S STRUGGLES FOR SELF-DETERMINATION

INDIGENOUS PEOPLE'S STRUGGLES FOR SELF - DETERMINATION

Prakash Louis

GYAN

Indigenous People's Struggles for Self-Determination

ISBN : 978-81-212-1159-8

Published in 2012 in India by
Gyan Publishing House
23, Main Ansari Road, Daryaganj,
New Delhi - 110002
Phones : 23282060, 23261060
Fax : (011) 23285914
E-mail: books@gyanbooks.com
website: gyanbooks.com

Laser Type Setting : Rajender Vashist, Delhi
Printed at : Chawla Offset Printers, Delhi

Dedicated to
the Indigenous Peoples all over the world
who continue to wage a relentless war
to uphold their lives, dignity, rights
and above all, their right to
self-determination.

This book in a special way is dedicated to
late Dr. Ram Dayal Munda who
nationalised the Indigenous Peoples' issues
and internationalised the Adivasis'/Tribals'
issues.

Contents

PART III: INTERNATIONAL FINANCE INSTITUTIONS AND INDIGENOUS PEOPLES

PART IV: OTHER INITIATIVES

Preface

Indigenous peoples are communities, and nations who claim a historical continuity and cultural affinity with societies endemic to their original territories that developed prior to exposure to the larger connected civilisation associated with western culture. These societies, therefore, consider themselves distinct from societies of the majority cultures that have contested their cultural sovereignty and self-determination. Other related terms for indigenous peoples include aborigines (aboriginal people, native people, first people, fourth world cultures and autochthonous). "Indigenous peoples" may often be used in preference to these or other terms as a neutral replacement, where such terms may have taken on negative or pejorative connotations by their prior association and use. It is the preferred term in use by the United Nations and its subsidiary organisations.

In the last two decades the issues of the indigenous peoples have come to the fore. It is not that before that this issue was not discussed. But from late 1980s onwards, there have been consistent and systematic attempts to highlight the situation of the indigenous people. In the recent past, there have been more and more efforts to focus on the plight of the indigenous peoples. Along with this, there is also the attempt to foreground the various attempts made by the indigenous peoples to resist the discrimination and exploitation they are subjected to and also to assert their right for self-determination.

It is expedient to state at the outset that there is no commonly agreed definition of the term 'indigenous peoples'. The government of India adamantly rejects the use of the term 'indigenous' for any of the people living within its boundary. It is argued by the government of India that the complex and age-old history of migration and exchange and mixing of cultural and physical traits makes it impossible to distinguish any group as 'indigenous' in relation to other groups; therefore everyone in India has to be considered indigenous. Irrespective of the denial mode adapted by the Indian Government, *adivasis* (original inhabitants) and Tribals (officially called the Scheduled Tribes) of India prefer to call themselves indigenous peoples.

Taking into account all these issues, an effort is made in this book to present the various issues of the indigenous peoples as it has unfolded itself over the last three to four decades. Here an attempt is made to examine the issues and struggles of the indigenous peoples from the various efforts made by them. Though the first selection of this compilation talks about Kari-Oca Conference held in Brazil in 1992, the struggles of the indigenous peoples are centuries older than this period. What we have documented in this book is only those that are recorded and available for public use. But the initiatives by the indigenous peoples go as early as they came in contact with the so-called modern civilisation or colonisers.

While the study of the tribals of India has gained some attention in the last three decades, the issues of the indigenous peoples continue to remain unattended by the social scientists. This book is an attempt to foreground the issues of the indigenous peoples from their perspective and approach. It is also an attempt to invite the intelligentsia of India and South Asia to engage in this important arena of inquiry so as to contribute in the upholding of the indigenous peoples' struggle for self-determination.

I am grateful to many individuals and institutions for their support in bringing out this book. First of all, I am grateful to the libraries of Indian Social Institute, New Delhi and Bengaluru from where, I got some relevant documents for this book. I thank late Smitu Kothari with whom I had been discussing about the issues of the indigenous peoples. It is to be noted here that Smitu attended the Latin American gathering of indigenous and tribal leaders and their allies at Mexico City, 6-9 December, 2003. I am grateful to Fidelis Tirkey who provided some of the documents from the Documentation Department of Indian Social Institute, New Delhi. Above all, I thank all those who began and maintain the websites from where I downloaded some of the documents for preparing this compilation.

I am grateful to Gyan Publishing House for bringing out the book in a record time. There are many others whom I am indebted to for bringing out this book. If not for their support and guidance, this book would not have seen the light of the day. To everyone, I extend 'thanks' from a grateful heart of course, the mistakes are due to my own limitations.

On 16 November 2010, the General Assembly adopted a resolution on indigenous peoples' issues. In this resolution, the General Assembly decided to organise a World Conference on Indigenous Peoples in 2014. It is hoped that declaring International Indigenous Peoples' Year and Decade or organising World Conference would ensure the dignity, rights and life of the people. Hope all these efforts would lead to the self-determination of the indigenous peoples.

Prakash Louis

Introduction

In the last two decades, the issues of the indigenous peoples have come to the fore. It is not that this issue was not discussed before; but from late 80s onwards, there have been consistent and systematic attempt to highlight the situation of the indigenous people. In the recent past, there have been more and more efforts to focus on the plight of the indigenous peoples. Along with this, there is also the attempt to foreground the various attempts made by the indigenous peoples to resist the discrimination and exploitation they are subjected to, and also to assert their right for self-determination. It is expedient to state the fact that there is no commonly agreed definition of the term 'indigenous peoples'.

Indigenous peoples are people, communities, and nations who claim a historical continuity and cultural affinity with societies endemic to their original territories that developed prior to exposure to the larger connected civilisation associated with western culture. These societies, therefore, consider themselves distinct from societies of the majority culture/s that have contested their cultural sovereignty and self-determination. Other related terms for indigenous peoples include aborigines (aboriginal people, native people, first people, fourth world cultures and autochthonous). 'Indigenous peoples' may often be used in preference to these or other terms as a neutral replacement, where such terms may have taken on negative or pejorative connotations by their prior association and use. It is the preferred term in use by the United Nations and its subsidiary organisations.

According to the **International Working Group for Indigenous Affairs** (IWGIA) *"Although indigenous peoples are quite diverse they, nevertheless, have three important and related aspects in common. First, there is the cultural aspect* *which binds them to the term 'peoples'. We are dealing here with a group which, because of a common history, culture, affiliation to an area of land, language, etc. considers and feels itself one entity – a people or a nation. Secondly, there is the notion of a common territory. Finally, there is the political aspect which recognises that indigenous peoples or nations have at one time been deprived of the possibilities to control their own affairs, territory, wealth and prospects for development. Their members are often marginalised and excluded from political decision-making processes; and their collective and national rights to land, water and culture are not recognised by the dominating and governing groups of the state"* (IWGIA 1994, Indigenous World 1993-1994, Copenhagen).

The government of India adamantly rejects the use of the term 'indigenous' for any of the people living within its boundary. It is argued that the complex and age-old history of migration and exchange and mixing of cultural and physical traits makes it impossible to distinguish any group as 'indigenous' in relation to other groups; therefore, everyone in India has to be considered indigenous. Irrespective of the denial mode adapted by the Indian Government, adivasis and Tribals of India prefer to call themselves indigenous peoples.

What indigenous activists in India, their local and outside supporters, some Indian and foreign academics as well as overseas development agencies like the World Bank refer to when they speak of indigenous peoples in India roughly corresponds to what, in official parlance, are called 'Scheduled Tribes'. Contrary to the government's position, the so-called 'Scheduled Tribes' possess many characteristics which, according to internationally accepted definitions (such as ILO Convention 169, the Martínez-Cobo report or World Bank Operational Directive, No. 4.20) sufficiently qualify them to be called 'indigenous peoples'. More important, and still not recognised by the Indian state, is what **Karlsson** has stressed in a recent article: that *"the concept 'indigenous peoples' is clearly a political fact in India today. Tribal communities increasingly identify and mobilise as indigenous peoples (or as adivasis) to claim rights over land and resources. The global discourse on indigenousness apparently resonates with or captures central features of tribal predicaments and aspirations"*.

According to the United Nations, the world has at least 5,000 indigenous groups with a total population of 300 million living in more than 70 countries. Around 70% of them live in Asia, 84 million of them in India. Despite these numbers, the UN has never defined the word 'indigenous'. The concept was born in the Americas, Australia and New Zealand where a clear line divides them from the continents' later conquerors. In South Asia, the majority population has lived in the area for millennia. As a result, there is difference of opinion on who is indigenous to these countries (Walter Fernandes: 2008, p. 2).

As stated above, there are some 5,000 different indigenous and tribal peoples living in around 70 countries. The majority of them are in rural areas and forest regions. They differ from each other in their cultural identity, economic organisation, social and religious practices, environmental milieu and the degree and nature of their relationship to national political and economic system. But they share at least one common characteristic, that is, they are at the bottom of social order in the society and country they live in. They are the most discriminated and exploited segment of the population of any country.

The United Nations Working Group on Indigenous Populations points out that the indigenous peoples have been deprived of human rights and fundamental freedoms, thereby affecting their right to development 'according to their own needs and interests'. There also exist extreme forms of exploitation by officials, traders and contractors (Dev Nathan: 2004, p. 20).

Indigenous peoples confront a diverse range of issues associated with their status and interaction with other cultural groups, as well as changes in their inhabited environment. Some challenges are specific to particular groups; however, other challenges are commonly experienced by the indigenous people all over the world. There are studies which indicate that the situation of some of the indigenous people in some countries has comparatively improved. But there are also studies which state that the condition of the indigenous peoples in many parts of the world is deplorable.

The issues that are crucial in the discussion of the indigenous peoples include distinct cultural and linguistic identity, preservation of cultural and social practices, geographical location, land and resource rights, ownership and access to natural resources, development according to their socio-cultural milieu, political determination and autonomy. The administrative systems that the indigenous people had developed over the years were also brought under stress due to the superimposing of the alien administrative structures. Along with these, the historical exploitation and genocide have become points for discussion.

Let us take the example of indigenous peoples of India, and discuss some of the issues that affect them. According to the tribal ethos, they are part of the entire *jal, jungle aur zamin* (water, forest and land) and their ancestors are also part of them. These natural resources constitute the very lifeline of the tribal population. These resources make up the economic, social, cultural, political and religious universe of the tribal community. The tribal women in a special way had a say and control over these resources. With the introduction of development-induced displacement, vast segment of the tribal population are displaced from their natural habitats and also are subjected to innumerable forms of exploitation. While land alienation and displacement have become integral part of tribal history, rehabilitation of them does not seem to be part of the national agenda.

A careful examination of displacement and rehabilitation of the tribals at the all-India level unravels this fact that among the 21.3 million population who are displaced, more than 40% are tribals. Out of the 21.3 million who were displaced, only 5.4 million were resettled. Among the total resettled just about 25% of the tribals are resettled. Thus, from this data it becomes clear that though the tribals constitute only 8% of the population of the national population, more than 40% among them are displaced. But when it comes to resettlement, just about 25% of the displaced are resettled. This clearly indicates the bias against the tribal communities in India. Thus, the tribals who are used to live in symbiotic relationship with nature are reduced to be aliens in their own land. Women in a special way loose out control over resources and this increases their burden in terms of finding fuel, fodder and food (Prakash Louis 2003: 191-204).

The interaction between indigenous and non-indigenous societies throughout history has been complex, ranging from outright conflict and subjugation to some degree of mutual benefit and cultural transfer. But in most cases, the interaction has been one of trying to assimilate and thus disintegrate the indigenous peoples. In the name of 'mainstreaming' the indigenous people, they were and are subjugated by the so-called 'modern society'.

In such discriminating and exploiting situation, the indigenous people did not lie low. At different intervals, they rose against their exploiters and oppressors. Individuals and communities tried to resist the invasion of the non-indigenous people and tried to uphold their culture, religion, social structure, resources, dignity, freedom and rights. In spite of being treated as primitive, minority, etc., the indigenous people maintained their socio-cultural values and principles, and progressed further. They also kept on struggling against all the forces and factors which were against them.

Written records bear testimony to the fact that the indigenous people fought against the colonisers and the native rulers. Indian history bears testimony to the fact that as early as in 1778, there broke out the revolt of the Pahariya Sirdars of Chotanagpur (present day Jharkhand) against the British colonisers. Similar struggles and movements are recorded in other parts of the world. The indigenous people also raised the issue of their dignity, freedom and rights in the international forums. All these forced the UN to declare the UN Year of the Indigenous Populations from October 1992 to 8 December 1993, during the anniversary of the Universal Declaration of the Human Rights.

The indigenous movement that culminated in the UN Decade can be traced back to 1923 when the Cayuga Chief, Deskaheh, a representative of the Iroquois of Ontario in Canada went to the League of Nations to represent the 'Six Nations of the Great River'. He carried a passport issued by the 'authority of his people'. Already before this in 1921, the General

Body of the International Labour Organisation (ILO) showed concern for indigenous workers, who were among the most exploited. In 1926, ILO created a 'Committee of Experts on Native Labour' and in 1936 its Governing Body adopted Convention No. 59 'Concerning the Regulation of Certain Special Systems of Recruiting Workers'. In 1939 it adopted Convention No 64 'Concerning the Regulation of Certain Special Systems of Recruiting Workers'.

However, the real indigenous rights movement began only with decolonisation after the Second World War. Autonomy movements began in several independent countries that are in reality federations of many nations. The Naga Nationalist Struggle is one of the best known among them. Most such movements were in Latin America whose indigenous populations were feeling doubly exploited. On the one hand, foreign companies controlled their wealth and on the other hand, the national elite collaborated with those foreign corporations. A specific contribution of the Second World War was the awareness of genocide. In the context of the Nazi programme of the Jews, Gypsies and Poles, many indigenous communities of the Americas asked questions about the genocide of their own ancestors. Additionally, European indigenous peoples began to become more aware of their rights.

These movements created heightened awareness in some international organisations, especially ILO whose mandate is protection of workers' rights. Since indigenous workers were among the most exploited, their welfare too was initially entrusted to this organisation. Awareness of possible genocide of indigenous populations added to the concern about their exploitation. The result was ILO convention of 107 of 1957 'concerning the Protection and Integration of Indigenous and Other Tribal and Semi-Tribal Populations in Independent Countries'. Its focus was protection and integration but its approach was more assimilationist than integrationist.

These steps eventually lead to the UN Decade of the Indigenous Peoples. Because of the ILO conventions and the struggle of the indigenous peoples, by the 1980s, the indigenous issue began to be perceived as human rights issue. Since any talk of their minority rights was stalled at the UN General

Assembly, in 1971 Augusto Willemsen Diaz of Guetamala, who was on the UN staff in Geneva, shifted his focus to the UN mandate to prevent any form of discrimination. In 1971, he got the UN Sub-Commission on Prevention of Discrimination and Protection of Minorities to commission a study on discrimination against indigenous peoples. In the mid-1970s, two non-governmental organisations of the Americas were granted accreditation with the UN Economic and Social Commission. Since the awareness of indigenous rights was growing also in Europe, two European organisations were founded in the 1970s viz. the Work Group for Indigenous Affairs at the University of Copenhagen and Survival International in London. The first NGO international conference on indigenous affairs was held in 1977. From the 1980s, Norway and Holland gave importance to the indigenous issue in their international relations.

These movements would eventually coalesce as the centenary of Christopher Columbus in 1992 approached. That became the immediate event leading to the Decade of the Indigenous Peoples, 1995-2004. While the white populations of the Americas wanted to celebrate the Columbus' voyage and the fifth centenary of the 'discovery' as a triumph, the descendants of the original inhabitants who were subjugated by the conquerors asked: 'Who discovered whom?' They observed it as an anniversary of their oppression and demanded that they be recognised as the original inhabitants of the conquered continents because they have been deprived of their right to be fully human.

In response to this, the UN declared the UN Year of the Indigenous Populations from October 1992 to 8 December, 1993, the anniversary of the Universal Declaration of the Human Rights. However, it was felt that the communities that had been suppressed for five centuries deserved more support than the observance of a single year. As the refusal of the original Native Americans showed, they were becoming aware of their right to be human. The very nomenclature 'indigenous' is a result of that awakening. In Australia, the awakening of the Aborigines symbolised by the Mabo case through which indigenous peoples challenged the right of non-indigenous peoples over many territories of the country. The Australian high court upheld this contention.

Thus, the declaration of the Indigenous Decade 1995-2004 is a tribute to the original inhabitants and 'conquered peoples' who were demanding their right to be human. The goal of the decade was to "strengthen international cooperation for the solution of the problems faced by indigenous peoples in the areas of human rights, culture, environment, development, education and health. Its theme is 'Indigenous People: Partnership in Action'. It was hoped that indigenous leaders and friends would be able to use the decade both to help their communities to become aware of their identity and make other communities aware of their situation. In order to reinforce this effort, a second decade of the Indigenous Peoples was declared in 2005-2014 (Walter Fernandes: 2008, p 2-4).

Irrespective of all the efforts made by the indigenous peoples, their friends, many institutions and organisations that address the issues of the indigenous peoples, human rights institutions and the UN bodies, the condition of the indigenous peoples continues to be extremely precarious and vulnerable. Most of them continue to be marginalised, exploited and oppressed by the non-indigenous groups. Thus, the story of the indigenous peoples' world over, is one of exploitation and discrimination and also struggle for survival, dignity, freedom and self-determination. Two perspectives from India highlight the exploitation and assertion of the indigenous peoples of India and also of the world.

After taking into account the discrimination and exploitation suffered by the tribals, Ram Dayal Munda, the ideologue of the tribals of India and also the former President of the International Confederation of Indigenous and Tribal Peoples, India calls for a coordinated efforts to bring together awakened groups of people. These coordination efforts will have to be accomplished at all levels – ethnic, social, linguistic, religious, political, economic and gender. Unless this is systematically undertaken, the tribal movement itself will wither away. Thus, with the arrival of tribal states, if the tribal movement for self-determination, preservation of their *jal, jungle* and *zamin*, socio-cultural assertion and tribal self-rule withers away, then the tribals would be annihilated once and for all from the tribal region (Ram Dayal Munda, n.a).

The Final Declaration of the National Assembly of Tribal, Indigenous and Adivasi Peoples held in New Delhi on 21 September 2004 highlights some of the Non-Negotiable Principles for a National Policy for Tribal, Indigenous and Adivasi Peoples.[1]

(i) Principles of Fundamental Respect of Difference, by which is implied the acceptance and respect for different societies with our distinct identity, culture, ethos and ways of life.

(ii) Principles of Recognition of the Natural and Juridical Socio-Economic, Cultural and Political Rights of Tribal, Indigenous and *Adivasi* communities by which is implied the recognition of the Rights to :

(a) life and livelihood with dignity.

(b) land, including our ancestral homelands and command over our natural resources, and protection and regeneration of natural resources in our lands.

(c) express and uphold our distinct identities, cultures, ethos and ways of life.

(d) protect and advance our traditional systems of governance, customary laws and jurisprudence.

(e) protect and further our own cultures and civilisations.

(f) self-governance and determination of our development and our futures.

(iii) Principles of Participation and Primacy of the People in formulation of laws and policies that affect us.

(iv) Principles of Responsibility of the State to safeguard the rights and genuine aspirations of our peoples and ensure their fulfillment.

(v) Principles of Responsibility of the State to rectify historical injustices and restore our legitimate rights.

This book 'Indigenous People's Struggles for Self-Determination' is an attempt to foreground the various initiatives of the indigenous peoples to determine their life, resources, dignity, rights, etc. Along with these, we also present the interaction between the indigenous peoples and the United Nations, an international organisation which is supposed to highlight, defend and protect the rights, dignity and life of all, especially the indigenous people. Above all, it is a long drawn out struggle for self-determination. We have also presented two documents, one of World Bank and the other of Asian Development Bank to focus on the perception and approach of international financial institutions. A select bibliography is given at the end so as to invite the reader to probe further into one of the most intriguing and inspiring struggle for self-determination.

Note

1. Final Declaration of the National Assembly of Tribal, Indigenous and *Adivasi* Peoples. This National Assembly was held in New Delhi from 21-23 September 2004 to review and respond to the National Draft Tribal Policy. Due to the protest from various tribal and indigenous peoples and communities, the then Government of India shelved this draft policy.

Part I
Initiatives by Indigenous Peoples

Introduction

In the general introduction to this compilation, we have spelt out the situation of the indigenous people and their assertion for self-determination. We also briefly discussed the various efforts made by the indigenous people and others to highlight the issue of the indigenous people. In this section, we will present a panoramic view of the various initiatives undertaken by the indigenous people themselves. Some of these are efforts made by the indigenous people themselves and some are in response to the processes initiated by others. We are focusing only on the efforts made in the last two decades, that is, from 1990 to 2010.

As early as 1992, indigenous people organised the Kari-Oca Conference in Brazil. Over 650 Indigenous representatives from the five continents, organised into 92 different Indigenous organisations, adopted a 109 point Indigenous Peoples' Earth Charter containing the conclusions of the Kari-Oca Conference and the demands of the Indigenous Peoples. This Charter forms part of a document containing the Kari-Oca Declaration and the various resolutions passed during the conference.

The Charter contains environmental demands to state governments to cease all uses of nuclear material (47) and that Indigenous lands must not be used for testing or dumping of nuclear products (49). Indigenous Peoples should make guidelines for environmental groups, who, in many instances, are more concerned about insects than human beings (40).

On Bio-diversity and Conservation, the Charter demands that the indigenous peoples cannot be included as part of a bio-diversity, which pretends to be maintained for scientific and folkloric purposes (59). On Human Rights and International Law, points 6 and 36 of the document state that the concept of *terra nullus* should be erased from law books and from international law usage.

Further, the Charter also demands that the indigenous peoples have inalienable rights to their lands and resources (33). Parks must not be created at the expense of indigenous peoples; there is no way to separate indigenous peoples from their lands (41). The reason given by the participants of Kari-Oca Conference is that 'Indigenous peoples were placed upon our Mother the Earth by the Creator. We belong to the land. We cannot be separated from our lands and territories' (31). Thus, land is not just the livelihood provider for the indigenous peoples but is much more, and it is through land they are related to the creator.

What the so-called mainstream or modern society fails miserably to understand is that it is the indigenous peoples who are the saviours of Mother Earth. In the Preamble to the Kari-Oca Declaration they articulate it well. *"We continue building and formulating our united commitment to save our Mother Earth"*. It is not that the so-called modern society does not understand this but it pretends not to understand and accept this truth so that it can continue to exploit the indigenous peoples.

The Indian Confederation of Indigenous and Tribal Peoples (ICITP) held its Second General Assembly in November 1993 in Delhi. From the name of this confederation itself, one becomes aware of the fact that the indigenous peoples of India use both the domestic term tribal and international term indigenous peoples. Moreover, to assert their rightful demand as indigenous peoples, they have been waging a battle. The indigenous people of India do not want the constitutional term *anusuchit janjati* (Scheduled Tribe) imposed upon them by the colonial rulers and followed by the native rulers even now.

The ICITP was one time very active and used to participate in the Working Group on a Permanent Forum for Indigenous

Peoples in the 90s and in the Permanent Forum for Indigenous Peoples after 2000. The **Confederation** declared, *"We, the tribals of India, are proud of the fact that we are the first inhabitants of our Motherland. We have contributed much to the culture, history and heritage of India. However, little respect is today shown to our culture, social systems, political structures and economy. Efforts are made to integrate us into the mainstream society as a low caste, though traditionally we have lived in an egalitarian and casteless society in which women had a fairly high status. Our culture is looked down upon and the dominant culture, with its caste-based inequalities and women's subordination is imposed on us".*

The Confederation has been demanding for indigenous status, though the Indian government does not recognise this. It opposes deforestation, land alienation and displacement. It also demanded that the traditional administrative system of the indigenous peoples be respected instead of imposing alien forms of government. Finally, the confederation demanded for social, cultural, economic and political self-determination.

One of the most active and effective groups at the Women's NGO Forum in the UN Fourth World Conference on Women in Beijing were the indigenous women. They organised activities such as workshops and cultural events in the Indigenous Women's Tent. After many days of discussion, they also issued a Beijing Declaration of Indigenous Women which comprehensively sets out the major global and national causes of their plight. The Declaration, signed by 118 indigenous groups from 27 southern and northern countries, is presented here as the third section of Part I.

The indigenous women clearly and categorically spell out the discrimination they are subjected to and also their resolve to fight discrimination and also to preserve Mother Earth. *"We, the women of the original peoples of the world have struggled actively to defend our rights to self-determination and to our territories, which have been invaded and colonised by powerful nations and interests. We have been and are continuing to suffer from multiple oppressions; as Indigenous peoples, as citizens of colonised and neo-colonial countries, as women, and as members of the poorer classes of society. In spite of this, we have been and continue to protect, transmit, and develop our Indigenous Cosmo vision, our science and technologies, our arts and culture, and our Indigenous socio-political economic systems, which are in harmony with the natural laws of mother earth."*

The indigenous women present in the Beijing Conference also spoke against the colonisation, marginalisation and discrimination of the indigenous peoples, and demanded for right to equal political participation. The women also resolved to work with non-indigenous women's organisations to implement a realistic plan of solidarity.

It needs to be stated here that about 60 indigenous women from different parts of the world participated at the 49th Session of the Commission on the Status of Women in March 2005 in New York, where the review and evaluation of the Beijing Declaration and Platform for Action took place. Indigenous women participated in two official panels and six side events, held two press conferences, attended a week-long seminar on international issues, adopted a declaration and proposed a resolution on indigenous women and girls that was finally adopted at the Commission on the Status of Women. The resolution, the first on indigenous women at the CSW, highlights their rights and specific needs, including regarding poverty and violence, and was considered a big achievement of the indigenous women's work. Thus, the indigenous women have not given up their struggle for life, dignity, liberty and rights.

TRIPS or the Agreement on Trade Related Aspects of Intellectual Property Rights is an international agreement administered by the World Trade Organisation (WTO) that sets down minimum standards for intellectual property regulations in 1994. Under this intellectual property right, it appears that the WTO wants to regulate ownership of intellectual property, in reality the WTO becomes the policeman to impose new regimes. Within a year after the imposition of TRIPS, the indigenous peoples opposed this saying, that some provisions of the agreement will further denigrate and undermine our rights to our cultural and intellectual heritage, our plant, animal, and even human genetic resources and discriminate against our indigenous ways of thinking and behaving. The indigenous peoples who met in Geneva in 1999 resolved their commitment to sustain the struggle to have their rights to their intellectual and cultural heritage and their lands and resources promoted and protected.

Once again in 1999, the indigenous peoples gathered during the Third Ministerial Meeting of the World Trade Organisation in Seattle to express their concern over how the WTO is destroying Mother Earth and the cultural and biological diversity. This document has come to be known as 'Indigenous Peoples' Seattle Declaration'. In this, the indigenous peoples stated that trade liberalisation and export led development, which are the basic principles on which policies promoted by the WTO are based, were creating extremely negative impacts on the lives of indigenous peoples.

In their opinion, the WTO agreements were undermining their right to self- determination, their sovereignty as peoples, the constructive treaties and agreements that indigenous peoples had negotiated with the states in which they lived. In this important declaration, indigenous peoples describe the serious impacts of these agreements on their communities, and ask the WTO to consider this problem urgently and demanding that:

- an urgent social and environmental justice analysis be undertaken to look into the cumulative effects of these Agreements on indigenous peoples.
- a review of the Agreements is undertaken to address the inequalities and imbalance that adversely affect indigenous peoples.

The Declaration also includes a large number of concrete proposals in relation to the Agreement on Agriculture, service and investment liberalisation and the TRIPS Agreement. The Seattle Declaration also calls for sustainable lifestyles and cultures, a transformed society where justice, equality and sustainability would prevail.

The next section deals with the Declaration of the First International Forum of Indigenous Peoples on Climate Change, held in Lyon, France, in 2000. In this forum, the indigenous peoples clearly articulate their perspective and concerns of climate change. The forum asserted that, 'we, the indigenous peoples, have historically played an active role in the conservation of eco-systems crucial to the prevention of climate change such as forests, wetlands and coastal and marine areas". Thus, while the so-called modern society began to speak of climate change much late, the indigenous people have been engaged in protecting the earth from climate change.

Not only this, the indigenous people have been speaking against the devastating development model of the west. They argued, "Long ago, our sciences foretold of the severe impacts of Western 'development' models based on indiscriminate clear-cutting, oil exploitation, mining, carbon-emitting industries, permanent organic pollutants and the insatiable consumption of the industrialised countries. Today, these unsustainable models threaten the very life of Mother Earth and the lives of all of us who are her children." The indigenous peoples also demanded that it is not just the climate change but the recognition and establishment of all the fundamental rights of the indigenous peoples is also equally important.

Ten years after the Kari Oca Conference held in Brazil in 1992, the indigenous peoples met at Kimberley, South Africa in 2002 to discuss about sustainable development. Kimberley Conference of the indigenous peoples was organised at the same time when the World Summit on Sustainable Development was organised by the United Nations in Johannesburg, South Africa. When the United Nations General Assembly authorised holding the World Summit on Sustainable Development, it was hardly a secret that progress in implementing sustainable development has been extremely disappointing since the 1992 Earth Summit at Rio, with poverty deepening and environmental degradation worsening. What the world wanted, the General Assembly said, was not a new philosophical or political debate but rather, a summit of actions and results.

The indigenous people who met at this occasion in Kimberley once again reaffirmed the Kari Oca Declaration and the Indigenous Peoples' Earth Charter. While the UN conference deliberated on sustainable development, the indigenous peoples discussed about the indigenous perspectives for development. They declared, *"We have the right to determine and establish priorities and strategies for our self -development and for the use of our lands, territories and other resources. We demand that free, prior and informed consent must be the principle of approving or rejecting any project or activity affecting our lands, territories and other resources".*

This conference also reaffirmed the indigenous peoples' right to self-determination and also to own, to control and manage their ancestral lands and territories, waters and other resources. They, in clear and categorical terms said that economic globalisation constitutes one of the main obstacles for the recognition of the rights of indigenous peoples.

It is expedient to state here that the United Nations is organising a conference on sustainable development in 2012, that is, ten years after the World Summit on Sustainable Development and twenty years after Earth Summit at Rio. Hence, the summit is referred to as Rio plus 20. It can be expected that the indigenous peoples too would organise parallel events to highlight their issues.

It is reported that an unprecedented round table discussion was held between indigenous leaders and World Bank senior management at World Bank headquarters on 17-18 October 2002. The meeting was hosted by the World Bank Vice President for Environmental and Socially Sustainable Development, Mr. Ian Johnson. Fifteen indigenous delegates from around the world participated in two days of discussions with bank management, staff, and members of the legal department regarding the revised Indigenous Peoples Policy and the obligations of the World Bank under international law, in particular human rights law. The indigenous participants were self-selected through a process facilitated by the International Alliance of Indigenous and Tribal Peoples. The indigenous delegates presented a statement listing their concerns about the process, and the content of the proposed Indigenous Peoples' Policy.

At the end of the meeting, Vice President Johnson publicly agreed to a number of longstanding demands regarding the on-going revision of the World Bank Indigenous Peoples Policy. The roundtable group, which included participants from a series of consultations with the WB, continues to engage the World Bank on issues of concern to indigenous peoples, and a second roundtable focused on the relationship of the IP Policy to international indigenous rights law is in the works.

One of the issues that the indigenous peoples emphasised was that the World Bank's mission of poverty reduction and sustainable development cannot be achieved without respecting and recognising the fundamental rights of the indigenous peoples. The indigenous peoples also demanded that when disbursing loans, the World Bank should keep its focus on following some of these laws.

We saw that whenever the United Nations organises any major conference, the indigenous peoples also organise parallel events to deliberate upon their state of affairs, highlight their issues, focus upon the discrimination and exploitation they are subjected to and also their efforts for self-determination. In the same way, when WTO organised its meetings, the indigenous peoples also organised parallel events. Thus, when the WTO organised its 5th Ministerial Conference in Caccun in Mexico in 2003, the indigenous peoples too organised their meeting in Cancun those days.

The indigenous peoples who gathered at Cancun forcefully stated that with the creation of WTO and with the continuing imposition of the structural adjustment policies of the World Bank and International Monetary Fund, their situation has turned from bad to worse. Hence, they demanded that the non-indigenous peoples recognise and protect the territorial and resource rights and the right to self-determination. Further, they demanded that the human-rights framework should underpin trade, investment, development and anti-poverty policies and programmes.

Going further, they called for the end of militarisation of indigenous peoples' communities and to stop the criminalisation of protest and resistance actions of indigenous peoples against destructive industries, projects and programmes. Thus, while the ministers who participate in WTO meeting discuss about economic issues and trade, the indigenous peoples bring to attention the human rights aspects.

In 2003, the indigenous peoples from the three continents gathered in Mexico and tried to evolve consensus among themselves on various issues. As stated in the declaration, it was also an attempt to evolve a perspective of the indigenous peoples on various issues. The gathering examined the present development paradigm. They asserted that in the present development paradigm, millions of people become unnecessary and disposable. Above all, they reiterated the 'we' sense among the indigenous peoples which brings solidarity among them. The following areas of consensus emerged among them: radical pluralism, personal dignity, radical democracy, create a new world, socialisation in contrast to privatisation and statisation, etc.

The next selection deals with the assessment of Asian Development Bank's (ADB) Forest Policy by Raja Devasish Roy. The writer is the Chief of the Chakma Administrative Circle in the Chittagong Hill Tracts (CHT), Bangladesh, an adviser to the Ministry of CHT Affairs, and is associated with various indigenous peoples' and development organisations, including the National Adivasi Coordination Committee, the Bangladesh Indigenous and Hill Peoples' Association for Advancement (BIHPAA), the Hill Tracts NGO Forum and Taungya. He is also an advocate at the Supreme Court of Bangladesh, Dhaka.

Raja Devasish Roy argues that despite provisions supporting the informed participation of indigenous peoples in ADB-funded interventions, that is, Indigenous Peoples and Forestry Policies, indigenous peoples have not been consulted substantively, or at all, before and during the formulation and implementation of policies and programmes in the forestry sector in many countries of the Asia-Pacific region, and especially in areas that are categorised as forests. Irrespective of all good intensions, the aforesaid interventions have led to many adverse consequences for indigenous peoples including (i) dislocation, (ii) deprivation from means of livelihood, (iii) human rights violations by foresters and law enforcing agencies, (iv) disruption of local culture and traditions, and (v) loss of biodiversity, among others.

The author pointedly argues that if there is a contradiction between the bank's *Indigenous Peoples' Policy* and another ADB policy or practice, the Indigenous Peoples policy will not necessarily prevail, and this can work to the detriment of indigenous peoples. Giving the example of Bangladesh, the author asserts that in the Bank's forestry sector support to the Government of Bangladesh, the provisions of the bank's forestry policy prevailed over its Indigenous Peoples policy. Similarly, another ADB-funded social forestry project in Bangladesh, which also affected indigenous peoples, was deemed to have paid little heed to the rights of women.

Devasish goes on to comment that a similar situation prevails in the case of the World Bank Indigenous Peoples' Policy, which bears striking similarities with the ADB's. Recent reforms to the World Bank's Indigenous Peoples' Policy – the replacement of OD 4.20 by OP 4.10/BP 4.10 – include many desirable provisions that respect indigenous peoples' rights. However, these appear to be merely recommendatory, rather than mandatory.

To rectify this situation, the author recommends that the policy itself be reviewed and reworked. But this would be of no use unless the indigenous peoples are part of this review process and outcome. There is the need for putting in place monitoring and evaluation mechanisms so as to ensure the implementation of the policies. But all these efforts would be of no use unless the international financial institutions also ensure the foregrounding of the rights of indigenous peoples in the domestic laws and implement them. Finally, in all the deliberations and negotiations with member countries, the Bank should include the representatives of indigenous peoples.

This is a statement from the International Indigenous Women's Forum on the MDGs calling on leaders to take specific steps during the MDG Review Summit in September 2007 to address the vast inequality and social inclusion faced by indigenous peoples, and indigenous women in particular. The International Indigenous Women Forum (FIMI), is a network of Indigenous women leaders, linked to networks of local, national and regional Asia, Africa and America. In this declaration, the indigenous women in clear and categorical term demand that **'No More Promises, A Call For Action'.**

The indigenous women gathered to review the implementation of **Millennium Development Goal** (MDG) declared that, *"We women of the indigenous peoples have struggled actively to defend our rights to self-determination and our territories have been invaded and colonised by powerful nations"*. Reiterating that the MDGs cannot be fulfilled without the full participation and empowerment of women, particularly indigenous women, and the respect of their human rights, the indigenous women stated that it is necessary to create and make available more opportunities for the exercise of their sexual and reproductive rights, the universal access to sexual, reproductive, and maternal health.

With regard to the implementation of MDG, the indigenous women assert, *"We call States and the UN System to make greater efforts to promote the full and effective participation of indigenous peoples with the greater participation of women, in designing, implementing and monitoring MDG-related programmes and policies that concern them or may affect them."* Thus, the indigenous women on their own right have been demanding their rights and inclusion.

1

Kari-Oca Declaration[1]

Preamble

The World Conference of Indigenous Peoples on Territory, Environment and Development (25–30 May 1992).

The Indigenous Peoples of the Americas, Asia, Africa, Australia, Europe, and the Pacific, united in one voice at Kari-Oca Villages, express our collective gratitude to the indigenous peoples of Brazil. Inspired by this historical meeting, we celebrate the spiritual unity of the indigenous peoples with the land and ourselves. We continue building and formulating our united commitment to save our Mother the Earth. We, the indigenous peoples, endorse the following declaration as our collective responsibility to carry our indigenous minds and voices into the future.

Declaration

We, the indigenous peoples, walk to the future in the footprints of our ancestors.

From the smallest to the largest living being, from the four directions, from the air, the land, and the mountains, the Creator has placed us, the indigenous peoples, upon our Mother the Earth.

> The footprints of our ancestors are permanently etched upon the land of our peoples.
>
> We, the indigenous peoples, maintain our inherent rights to self-determination.
>
> We have always had the right to decide our own forms

of government, to use our own laws to raise and educate our children, to our own cultural identity without interference.

We continue to maintain our rights as peoples despite centuries of deprivation, assimilation, and genocide.

We maintain our inalienable rights to our lands and territories, to all our resources — above and below — and to our waters. We assert our ongoing responsibility to pass these on to the future generations.

We cannot be removed from our lands. We, the indigenous peoples, are connected by the circle of life to our land and environments.

We, the indigenous peoples, walk to the future in the footprints of our ancestors.

Signed at Kari-Oca, Brazil,
on the 30th day of May, 1992

Indigenous Peoples' Earth Charter[2]

Human rights and international law

1. We demand the right to life.
2. International law must deal with the collective human rights of indigenous peoples.
3. There are many international instruments which deal with the rights of individuals, but there are no declarations to recognise collective human rights. Therefore, we urge governments to support the United Nations Working Group on Indigenous Peoples' (UNWGIP) Universal Declaration of Indigenous Rights, which is presently in draft form.
4. There exist many examples of genocide against indigenous peoples. Therefore, the convention against genocide must be changed to include the genocide of indigenous peoples.
5. The United Nations should be able to send indigenous peoples' representatives, in a peace-keeping capacity, into indigenous territories where conflicts arise. This would be done at the request and consent of the indigenous peoples concerned.
6. The concept of Terra Nullius must be eliminated from

international law usage. Many state governments have used internal domestic laws to deny us ownership of our own lands. These illegal acts should be condemned by the world.

7. Where small numbers of indigenous peoples are residing within state boundaries, so-called democratic countries have denied indigenous peoples the right of consent about their future, using the notion of majority rules to decide the future of indigenous peoples. Indigenous peoples' right of consent to projects in their areas must be recognised.
8. We must promote the term 'indigenous peoples' at all fora. The use of the term 'indigenous peoples' must be without qualifications.
9. We urge governments to ratify ILO Convention 169 to guarantee an international legal instrument for indigenous peoples (Group 2 only).
10. Indigenous peoples' distinct and separate rights within their own territories must be recognised.
11. We assert our rights to free passage through state-imposed political boundaries dividing our traditional territories. Adequate mechanisms must be established to secure this right.
12. The colonial systems have tried to dominate and assimilate our peoples. However, our peoples remain distinct despite these pressures.
13. Our indigenous governments and legal systems must be recognised by the United Nations, state governments, and international legal instruments.
14. Our right to self-determination must be recognised.
15. We must be free from population transfer.
16. We maintain our right to our traditional way of life.
17. We maintain our right to our spiritual way of life.
18. We maintain the right to be free from pressures from multinational (transnational) corporations upon lives and lands. All multinational (transnational) corporations which are encroaching upon indigenous lands should be reported to the United Nations Transnational Office.

19. We must be free from racism.
20. We maintain the right to decide the direction of our communities.
21. The United Nations should have a special procedure to deal with issues arising from violations of indigenous treaties.
22. Treaties signed between indigenous peoples and non-indigenous peoples must be accepted as treaties under international law.
23. The United Nations must exercise the right to impose sanctions against governments that violate the rights of indigenous peoples.
24. We urge the United Nations to include the issue of indigenous peoples in the agenda of the World Conference of Human Rights to be held in 1993. The work done so far by the United Nations Inter-American Commission of Human Rights and the Inter-American Institute of Human Rights should be taken into consideration.
25. Indigenous peoples should have the right to their own knowledge, language, and culturally appropriate education, including bicultural and bilingual education. Through recognising both formal and informal ways, the participation of family and community is guaranteed.
26. Our health rights must include the recognition and respect of traditional knowledge held by indigenous healers. This knowledge, including our traditional medicines and their preventive and spiritual healing power, must be recognised and protected against exploitation.
27. The World Court must extend its powers to include complaints by indigenous peoples.
28. There must be a monitoring system from this conference to oversee the return of delegates to their territories. The delegates should be free to attend and participate in international indigenous conferences.
29. Indigenous women's rights must be respected. Women must be included in all local, national, regional, and international organisations.

30. The above-mentioned historical rights of indigenous peoples must be guaranteed in national legislation.

Land and territories

31. Indigenous peoples were placed upon our Mother the Earth by the Creator. We belong to the land. We cannot be separated from our lands and territories.

32. Our territories are living totalities in permanent vital relation between human beings and nature. Their possession produces the development of our culture. Our territorial property should be inalienable, unceasable, and not denied title. Legal, economic, and technical back-up are needed to guarantee this.

33. Indigenous peoples' inalienable rights to land and resources confirm that we have always had ownership and stewardship over our traditional territories. We demand that these be respected.

34. We assert our rights to demarcate our traditional territories. The definition of territory includes space (air), land, and sea. We must promote a traditional analysis of traditional land rights in all our territories.

35. Where indigenous territories have been degraded, resources must be made available to restore them. The recuperation of those affected territories is the duty of the respective jurisdiction in all nation states, which cannot be delayed. Within this process of recuperation the compensation for the historical ecological debt must be taken into account. Nation states must revise in depth the agrarian, mining, and forestry policies.

36. Indigenous peoples reject the assertion of non-indigenous laws onto our lands; states cannot unilaterally extend their jurisdiction over our lands and territories. The concept of Terra Nullius should be forever erased from the law books of states.

37. We, as indigenous peoples, must never alienate our lands. We must always maintain control over the land for future generations.

38. If a non-indigenous government, individual, or corporation wants to use our lands, then there must be a formal

agreement which sets out the terms and conditions. Indigenous peoples maintain the right to be compensated for the use of their lands and resources.

39. Traditional indigenous territorial boundaries, including the waters, must be respected.
40. There must be some control placed upon environmental groups who are lobbying to protect our territories and the species within those territories. In many instances, environmental groups are more concerned about animals than human beings. We call for indigenous peoples to determine guidelines prior to allowing environmental groups into their territories.
41. Parks must not be created at the expense of indigenous peoples. There is no way to separate indigenous peoples from their lands.
42. Indigenous peoples must not be removed from their lands in order to make it available to settlers or other forms of economic activity on their lands.
43. In many instances, the numbers of indigenous peoples have been decreasing because of encroachment by non-indigenous peoples.
44. Indigenous peoples should encourage their peoples to cultivate their own traditional forms of products rather than to use imported exotic crops which do not benefit local peoples.
45. Toxic wastes must not be deposited in our areas. Indigenous peoples must realise that chemicals, pesticides, and hazardous wastes do not benefit the peoples.
46. Traditional areas must be protected against present and future forms of environmental degradation.
47. There must be a cessation of all uses of nuclear material.
48. Mining of products for nuclear production must cease.
49. Indigenous lands must not be used for the testing or dumping of nuclear products.
50. Population transfer policies by state governments in our territories are causing hardship. Traditional lands are lost and traditional livelihoods are being destroyed.

51. Our lands are being used by state governments to obtain funds from the World Bank, the International Monetary Fund, the Asian Pacific Development Bank, and other institutions, which have led to a loss of our lands and territories.
52. In many countries, our lands are being used for military purposes. This is an unacceptable use of the lands.
53. The coloniser governments have changed the names of our traditional and sacred areas. Our children learn these foreign names and start to lose their identity. In addition, the changing of the name of a place diminishes respect for the spirits which reside in those areas.
54. Our forests are not being used for their intended purposes. The forests are being used to make money.
55. Traditional activities, such as making pottery, are being destroyed by the importation of industrial goods. This impoverishes the local peoples.

Biodiversity and conservation

56. The Vital Circles are in a continuous interrelation in such a way that the change of one of its elements affects the whole.
57. Climatic changes affect indigenous peoples and all humanity. In addition, ecological systems and their rhythms are affected, which contributes to the deterioration of our quality of life and increases our dependency.
58. The forests are being destroyed in the name of development and economic gains without considering the destruction of ecological balance. These activities do not benefit human beings, animals, birds, and fish. The logging concessions and incentives to the timber, cattle, and mining industries affecting the ecosystems and the natural resources should be cancelled.
59. We value the efforts of protection of the Biodiversity but we reject being included as part of an inert diversity which pretends to be maintained for scientific and folkloric purposes.

60. The indigenous peoples' strategies should be kept in a reference framework for the formulation and application of national policies on environment and biodiversity.

Development strategies

61. Indigenous peoples must consent to all projects in our territories. Prior to consent being obtained, the peoples must be fully and entirely involved in any decisions. They must be given all the information about the project and its effects. Failure to do so should be considered a crime against the indigenous peoples. The person or persons who violate this should be tried in a world tribunal within the control of indigenous peoples set for such a purpose. This could be similar to the trials held after the Second World War.

62. We have the right to our own development strategies based on our cultural practices and with a transparent, efficient, and viable management and with economical and ecological viability.

63. Our development and life strategies are obstructed by the interests of the government and big companies and by the neoliberal policies. Our strategies have, as a fundamental condition, the existence of international relationships based on justice, equity, and solidarity between the human beings and the nations.

64. Any development strategy should prioritise the elimination of poverty, the climatic guarantee, the sustainable manageability of natural resources, the continuity of democratic societies, and the respect of cultural differences.

65. The Global Environmental Facility should assign at best 20 percent for indigenous peoples' strategies and programs of environmental emergency, improvement of life quality, protection of natural resources, and rehabilitation of ecosystems. This proposal in the case of South America and the Caribbean should be concrete in the indigenous development fund as a pilot experience in order to be extended to the indigenous peoples of other regions and continents.

66. The concept of development has meant the destruction of our lands. We reject the current definition of development as being useful to our peoples. Our cultures are not static and we keep our identity through a permanent recreation of our life conditions; but all of this is obstructed in the name of so-called developments.

67. Recognising indigenous peoples' harmonious relationship with Nature, indigenous sustainable development strategies and cultural values must be respected as distinct and vital sources of knowledge.

68. Indigenous peoples have been here since the time before time began. We have come directly from the Creator. We have lived and kept the Earth as it was on the First Day. Peoples who do not belong to the land must go out from the lands because those things (so called 'development" on the land) are against the laws of the Creator.

69.

    1. In order for indigenous peoples to assume control, management and administration of their resources and territories, development projects must be based on the principles of self-determination and self-management.
    2. Indigenous peoples must be self-reliant.

70. If we are going to grow crops, we must feed the peoples. It is not appropriate that the lands be used to grow crops which do not benefit the local peoples.

    1. Regarding indigenous policies, state government must cease attempts of assimilation and integration.
    2. Indigenous peoples must consent to all projects in their territories. Prior to consent being obtained, the peoples must be fully and entirely involved in any decisions. They must be given all the information about the project and its effects. Failure to do so should be considered a crime against indigenous peoples. The person or persons responsible should be tried before a world tribunal, with a balance of indigenous peoples set up for such a purpose. This

could be similar to the trials held after the Second World War.

71. We must never use the term 'land claims'. It is the non-indigenous peoples which do not have any land. All the land is our land. It is non-indigenous peoples who are making claims to our lands. We are not making claims to our lands.

72. There should be a monitoring body within the United Nations to monitor all the land disputes around the world prior to development.

73. There should be a United Nations conference on the topic of 'Indigenous Lands and Development'.

74. Non-indigenous peoples have come to our lands for the purpose of exploiting these lands and resources to benefit themselves, and to the impoverishment of our peoples. Indigenous peoples are victims of development. In many cases, indigenous peoples are exterminated in the name of a development program. There are numerous examples of such occurrences.

75. Development that occurs on indigenous lands, without the consent of indigenous peoples, must be stopped.

76. Development which is occurring on indigenous lands is usually decided without local consultation by those who are unfamiliar with local conditions and needs.

77. The Eurocentric notion of ownership is destroying our peoples. We must return to our own view of the world, of the land, and of development. The issue cannot be separated from indigenous peoples' rights.

78. There are many different types of so-called development: road construction, and communication facilities such as electricity, telephones. These allow developers easier access to the areas, but the effects of such industrialisation destroy the lands.

79. There is a worldwide move to remove indigenous peoples from their lands and place them in villages. The relocation from the traditional territories is done to facilitate development.

80. It is not appropriate for governments or agencies to move into our territories and to tell our peoples what is needed.
81. In many instances, the state governments have created artificial entities such as 'district council" in the name of the state government in order to deceive the international community. These artificial entities then are consulted about development in the area. The state government, then, claims that indigenous peoples were consulted about the project. These lies must be exposed to the international community.
82. There must be an effective network to disseminate material and information between indigenous peoples. This is necessary in order to keep informed about the problems of other indigenous peoples.
83. Indigenous peoples should form and direct their own environmental network.

Culture, science, and intellectual property

84. We feel the Earth as if we are within our mother. When the Earth is sick and polluted, human health is impossible. To heal ourselves, we must heal the Planet, and to heal the Planet, we must heal ourselves.
85. We must begin to heal from the grassroots level and work towards the international level.
86. The destruction of the culture has always been considered an internal, domestic problem within national states. The United Nation must set up a tribunal to review the cultural destruction of the indigenous peoples.
87. We need to have foreign observers come into our indigenous territories to oversee national state elections to prevent corruption.
88. The human remains and artifacts of indigenous peoples must be returned to their original peoples.
89. Our sacred and ceremonial sites should be protected and considered as the patrimony of indigenous peoples and humanity. The establishment of a set of legal and operational instruments at both national and international levels would guarantee this.

90. The use of existing indigenous languages is our right. These languages must be protected.
91. States that have outlawed indigenous languages and their alphabets should be censored by United Nations.
92. We must not allow tourism to be used to diminish our culture. Tourists come into the communities and view the people as if indigenous peoples were part of a zoo. Indigenous peoples have the right to allow or to disallow tourism within their areas.
93. Indigenous peoples must have the necessary resources and control over their own education systems.
94. Elders must be recognised and respected as teachers of the young people.
95. Indigenous wisdom must be recognised and encouraged.
96. The traditional knowledge of herbs and plants must be protected and passed onto future generations.
97. Traditions cannot be separated from land, territory, or science.
98. Traditional knowledge has enabled indigenous peoples to survive.
99. The usurping of traditional medicines and knowledge from indigenous peoples should be considered a crime against peoples.
100. Material culture is being used by the non-indigenous to gain access to our lands and resources, thus destroying our cultures.
101. Most of the media at this conference were only interested in the pictures which will be sold for profit. This is another case of exploitation of indigenous peoples. This does not advance the cause of indigenous peoples.
102. As creators and carriers of civilisations which have given and continue to share knowledge, experience, and values with humanity, we require that our right to intellectual and cultural properties be guaranteed and that the mechanism for each implementation be in favour of our peoples and studied in depth and implemented. This respect must include the right over genetic resources,

genebanks, biotechnology, and knowledge of biodiversity programs.

103. We should list the suspect museums and institutions that have misused our cultural and intellectual properties.

104. The protection, norms, and mechanisms of artistic and artisan creation of our peoples must be established and implemented in order to avoid plunder, plagiarism, undue exposure, and use.

105. When indigenous peoples leave their communities, they should make every effort to return to the community.

106. In many instances, our songs, dances, and ceremonies have been viewed as the only aspects of our lives. In some instances, we have been asked to change a ceremony or a song to suit the occasion; this is racism.

107. At local, national, and international levels, governments must commit funds to new and existing resources to education and training for indigenous peoples, to achieve their sustainable development, to contribute and to participate in sustainable and equitable development at all levels. Particular attention should be given to indigenous women, children, and youth.

108. All kinds of folkloric discrimination must be stopped and forbidden.

109. The United Nations should promote research into indigenous knowledge and develop a network of indigenous sciences.

Notes

1. The original text of the declaration and documents have been maintained fully. For the sake of convenience editing has been done in the Indian style but the meanings are not altered or changed.
2. Please note, for the purposes of the Declaration, and this statement, any use of the term ‘indigenous peoples” also includes tribal peoples.

2

Indian Confederation of Indigenous[1] and Tribal Peoples (ICITP)[2] Second General Assembly

Resolutions

We, the tribals of India, are proud of the fact that we are the first inhabitants of our motherland. We have contributed much to the culture, history and heritage of India. However, little respect is shown to our culture, social systems, political structures and economy today. Efforts are made to integrate us into the mainstream society as a low caste, though traditionally we have lived in an egalitarian and casteless society in which women had a fairly high status. Our culture is looked down upon and the dominant culture, with its caste-based inequalities and women's subordination is imposed on us. Our languages are not respected and none of them finds a place in the eighth schedule though languages spoken by a much smaller number of persons are given this status. Most of our tribes have been divided between different states of the Union, though for more than half a century some tribals, in Eastern India have been demanding an autonomous state within the Indian Union.

We live in resource-rich regions. Most forests and coalmines are in areas inhabited by us. Our land is blessed with rivers and other sources of water. These forests are our livelihood since much of our food and other needs come from them. We have, therefore, treated them as an environment. We have traditionally reserved them for posterity. But today they are being destroyed in the name of national development. We are thus deprived of our livelihood and are impoverished.

More and more major dams are built in the regions we live in. They displace millions of us. Coal and other mines displace more of us. Many industries are established in our habitat. They as well as wildlife sanctuaries displace many more of us. When test firing ranges and defence establishments are planned, priority seems to be given to building them in our regions. As a result, more than 40 per cent of the over 20 million persons displaced by development projects since 1950 are tribals, though we form only 7.85 per cent of the country's population. Fewer than 20 per cent of the persons thus displaced have been resettled till now.

As a result, a large number of us have been impoverished. Many of us have been forced to migrate away from our homes and work as daily wage, and even as bonded labourers. Our culture was based on the principles of keeping a balance between human and ecological needs and of preserving the natural resources for posterity. But today, our impoverishment forces us to cut forests either for sale as firewood or as labourers under timber contractors and smugglers. We have, thus, become only suppliers of cheap raw material and cheap labour of others. We do not get the benefits of development all its fruits are enjoyed by other communities far away. But we pay the price.

Tribal women are the worst sufferers. Displacement for development projects has deprived them of their land and forests from which much of our food came. They have today to walk much greater distances than in the past to collect the food and fodder we need. Deforestation has deprived us of the medicinal herbs. And women, who were the trustees of these resources among us, are further marginalised. Impoverishment forces many of our women to migrate to towns and cities as domestic servants. Many of them are also lured into prostitution.

After impoverishing us, the Government of India gives us some relief in the form of reservations and Integrated Tribal Development Plans. However, it is not prepared to deal with the causes of our impoverishment. Even these few relief measures are not implemented properly. Efforts are made to reduce our numbers or to deprive us of these benefits. For example, in many places non-tribals get bogus tribe certificates and make use of the benefits reserved for us. In other places, our name is changed during the census operations in order to deprive us of our Scheduled Status. For example, the Chile-Baraiks of Chotanagpur who are a Scheduled Tribe are mentioned in the census as Barail, which is a Rajput caste.

I. Indigenous Status

It is in this context that our demand to be recognised as the indigenous people of India has to be understood. Our economy, social systems, culture and political structures were built round these natural resources. Deprival of these resources and our impoverishment through deforestation and displacement and the attack on our livelihood has, therefore, caused a major crisis in our total life. We are forced to give up much of what once belonged to us. We certainly do not want to go back to the last century and remain unchanged. Abcve all we do not want to be museum pieces for the enjoyment of tourists. We would like to change, but on our terms, with respect for our traditions and culture. Our very identity is centered on these resources and we would like to maintain it since that is part of our self-respect and human rights.

That is where our demand to be recognised as the country's' indigenous people becomes meaningful. There are two international conventions concerning the indigenous populations, both of them of ILO. Convention 107 of 1957 takes an integrationist approach. Its perspective is that the indigenous peoples should be integrated into the mainstream culture and society. No respect is shown to our culture and lifestyle. The Government of India has ratified this Convention.

On the contrary, Convention 169 of 1989 is based on respect for the indigenous culture whose basis is sustainable development, conservation of the environment, egalitarian distribution of resources and respect for women. It also requires that the indigenous populations should not be displaced except under very strict norms to be adhered to. Their culture and social systems have to be safeguarded. Community resources have to be replaced and they have to be rehabilitated properly. The Government of India has not ratified this convention.

1. Therefore, we the tribals of india, gathered in new delhi for the second general assembly of the indian cofederation of indigenous and tribal peoples, demand that the government of india recognise us as the indigenous peoples of india.
2. We also demand that the government of india ratify without further delay, convention 169 of 1989 that respects our lifestyle and culture and adhere to its norms in dealing with us.
3. We also demand that indigenous languages and cultures be shown greater respect than is done now. Primary education should be in tribal languages. Our customary laws should be respected. Legal, religious and cultural systems that are foreign to our culture and ethos should not be imposed on us against our will.

II. Forests and Deforestation

Forests are our very livelihood. More than 50 per cent of our food comes from them. Our culture, social systems, political structures, economy and religion are centred round the forest. But today deforestation to provide raw material to industry, mining, major dams and wildlife sanctuaries destroy more of them. We are thus impoverished. Our culture is under attack and our identity is lost. Even the law gives us some rights in forests. But today more and more of them are being taken away from us. We are thus deprived of our livelihood. A total crisis is thus caused in our lives. It is not merely our economy but also our culture, society and religion that are under attack. Our very identity is being destroyed by these measures. We are treated like foreigners and religion that are under attack. Our very identity is being destroyed by these measures. We are treated like foreigners and encroachers in our own land, particularly in the forests where we have lived and which we have preserved for thousands of years. The Government, represented by its forest department, behaves like a landlord and we are treated like tenants at will with no rights whatever.

Also other forms of destruction affect us. For example, topsoil is not preserved while starting mining operations though the law demands that it be done. Land is not restored when mining operations are completed. Thus follow deforestation and land degradation, apart from pollution and other forms of destruction. The environmental crisis that follows is not a problem of tribals alone but of every community in India and of the whole human race. It is important to prevent it.

4. Therefore, we the tribals of india demand that forests be once again turned into a community asset.
5. Reforestation that has to be implemented on a war footing cannot be done without the involvement of the communities that have preserved them for centuries. We, therefore, demand that we be the main decision-makers in implementing it, in choosing the species to be planted. The organisation of work and in distributing its benefits. We shall certainly treat it as a resource put at the disposal of the country as a whole but with ourselves as equal partners in its benefits.
6. In this enterprise, we also demand that all forests degraded by mining and other operations be restored and that our communities be involved in this task. The forest department should provide technical assistance to people's communities.

III. Land Alienation, Land Acquisition and Displacement

(a) Land Alienation : Land is the very basis of tribal identity. The State has recognised this principle by declaring tribal land inalienable by law. But much of it is being alienated through fraudulent means in favour of non-tribal individuals and even public sector enterprises. Faulty tenancy legislation as well as the Land Acquisition Act 1894 has facilitated such a fraud on the tribals.

Every now and then the laws that are meant to protect us particularly Section 144,145 and 146 of

Cr PC are used against us tribals to deprive us of our land. Cases are filed against us in collusive title suits. The complicated and expensive procedures involved make it impossible for us to defend ourselves against these accusations. The judges on their part are ignorant of tribal customary laws.

7. It is, therefore, resolved that laws banning alienation of tribal lands should be strengthened. All tribal lands alienated from them through fraudulent means or through defective laws should be restored to them or to their descendants, and in the absence of descendants, to their village community.

   (b) **Land Acquisition and Displacement :** Tribals live in resource-rich regions. As such, they are considered only sources of cheap raw material and cheap labour. They are displaced with little consideration for their future, in order to exploit these resources. Often these projects are economically not viable. But this fact does not prevent the State from displacing more and more persons every year, a majority among them tribals. At least 10 per cent of all the tribals in the country have been displaced at least once during the last four decades. Impoverishment and marginalisation of the tribals is the consequence. This is a direct attack on our economy, social structures, culture and our very identity. Also the defence forces seem to give priority to having their bases in our areas. We can mention several of them like the MIG-HA1 factory and the Naval Armament Depot in Koraput district and many others both existing and being planned. The proposed Netarhat Firing Range in Chotanagpur alone will displace 156 villages with more one-lakh persons. Most of them are tribals. They include the Asurs who are an endangered tribe since fewer than a thousand of them live today. The Birhors are still forest gatherers and will not be able to adapt to life outside in a short time, even if they are resettled outside the forests.

8. The indian confederation of indigenous and tribal peoples, therefore, hereby resolves to take a strong stand on all forms of land alienation through displacement for development and other projects. The member organisations of icitp will join all tribal and other organisations and movements struggling against displacement and related forms of alienation of tribals from their livelihood and culture. We firmly oppose projects like the narmada schemes in Maharashtra, Madhya Pradesh and Gujarat, Subarnarekha, Koel-karo, Piparwar and Netarhat in Chotanagpur, Polavaram in Andhra Pradesh and others elsewhere that will displace hundreds and thousands of people, most of them tribals.

   In most cases, tribal and other lands are acquired in the name of public purpose. But the term public purpose has not been defined. So even the present law is abused by projects by acquiring lands in excess of their need. Often these lands are transferred to private individuals, particularly relatives of officials.

9. The members of icitp present here demand that public purpose be defined in an extremely restrictive manner to ensure that people are not displaced except in those rarest of rare cases when a serious social, economic and legal analysis done with the involvement of the people affected, shows the project to be inevitable.

   Moreover, the country that has displaced millions of people, a very large proportion of them tribals, does not as yet have a policy on rehabilitation. Fewer than 25 per cent of the more than 80 lakh tribals who have been displaced during the last four decades have been resettled. They get little or no compensation and very few jobs in the new projects are available to them. The little compensation they get is delayed inordinately and bribes are often demanded for it. Self-rehabilitation is impossible with that amount. Moreover, people are often displaced even against the present law, both by the government and private parties, without having first initiated land acquisition proceedings.

10. ICITP members present here protest against this process

of improverishment and dehumanisation. We demand that a policy and law on displacement be formulated immediately, to rehabilitate the tens of thousand who have been displaced and not resettled since the inception of the republic. All lands taken over till now without due legal process should be restored to their original owners or to their descendants, and if there are no descendants, to the village community. In those few cases where displacement is inevitable, adequate compensation and proper rehabilitation that take tribal structures and culture into consideration have to be an integral part of the project.

One way of imposing an alien culture on the tribals is to take only individually owned land into consideration, when in fact in the tradition of most tribal communities land, forests and other natural resources are held in common by the whole community. No common property is taken into consideration while calculating compensation.

11. The members of icitp present here, therefore, demand that the law recognise the communal ownership of land and other resources by the tribals in all the policies of the state. In those rarest of rare cases where displacement is inevitable, also the concept of compensation needs redefinition to include their total livelihood, and not merely individually held land.

A method the State that calls itself secular, has chosen to divide the oppressed is to make religion a criterion for applying the law of the State. Thus dalits who give up Hinduism are deprived of the SC reservations that are meant to compensate them for centuries of discrimination against them. In the case of the tribals, if they change their religion over to Hinduism, they are brought under the Hindu Succession Act and are deprived of their rights under their customary laws in the case of inheritance. These steps are violative of the fundamental rights as they are discriminatory against them on grounds of religion.

12. ICITP, therefore, protests against these attacks on tribal culture and demands that persons from the oppressed

communities be not deprived of any of their rights of privileges on grounds of religion. whatever religion they belong to, tribals should have the right to respect their own laws of inheritance.

IV. Constitutional and Administrative Measures

Most tribals have traditionally lived in an egalitarian society. Their administrative structures were controlled by the community rather than by higher authorities of the Government. Their *panchas* and other leaders appointed by the community through consensus exercised their power for the good of the whole tribe.

Even today, it would be possible to update and modernise this system and follow it to the benefit of the people. Articles 13 and 244 or the 5th Schedule of the constitution that apply to most tribal areas in Middle India and the Sixth Schedule that applies to the north-east make it possible. In reality, these clauses are not respected and no autonomy is granted to the tribals in running their internal affairs.

Besides, the country does not have a uniform policy for the tribals all over the country. For example, the constitutional safeguards are not respected. Tribes that are in the Schedule in one State are excluded from it in another. That, for example is the case with the Santals who are not included in the Schedule in Assam. Many others who have all the characteristics of tribals are not included in it. That would be the case of the Siddhis in Karnataka. In many other cases, persons from the upper castes fraudulently get the benefits of the schedule.

13. We, therefore, demand that a uniform policy be formulated for the tribals all over the country. A member of a scheduled tribe should be in the schedule wherever he/she is in the country. Fraudulent use of the privilege should be punished, since it cannot be done without the collection of government officials.

14. We also demand that a list of ethnic groups in danger of extinction be prepared and these groups be given special protection. Tribes like the siddhis who are not in the

schedule should be included in it. Local bodies of tribals can be used to identity these tribes.

15. The traditional systems of administration that have been dominant among the tribals should be respected and updated instead of imposing alien forms of government of them, self autonomous forms of administration permitted under the fifth and sixth schedules as well as other constitutional norms should be implemented with regard to the tribals.
16. Such self determination in the social, cultural, economic and political spheres should be an integral part of the new policy on the tribals since we consider it re-assertion of our rights as the indigenous peoples of india.

New Delhi October - November 1993

Notes

1. When the Government of India is denying the existence of indigenous peoples in India, to name this initiative as Indian Confederation of Indigenous and Tribal People, is indicative of the resolve to assert the existence and struggles of the indigenous peoples in India.
2. For the sake of maintaining the original text, both the content and format is kept as it was in the original text. Some editing was done and that has been done where necessary.

3

Beijing Declaration of Indigenous Women

NGO Forum, UN Fourth World Conference on Women, Huairou, Beijing, Peoples Republic of China

1. The earth is our mother. From her we get our life, and our ability to live. It is our responsibility to care for our mother and in caring for our mother we care for ourselves. Women, all females are a manifestation of Mother Earth in human form.
2. We, the daughters of mother earth, the indigenous women present at the NGO Forum of the UN Fourth World Conference on Women in Beijing, have come together to collectively decide what we can do to bring about a world which we would like our children and our children's children to live in. We acknowledge and build upon earlier declarations, which evolved from earlier meetings and conferences, like the 1990 Declaration of the Second International Indigenous Women's Conference, the Kari-Oca Declaration of 1992, and those of various regional conferences of Indigenous women, and the consultations and conferences done in preparation for this Beijing Conference.
3. This declaration is drafted in recognition of the existence of the UN Declaration of the International Decade of the World's Indigenous Peoples, the Draft Declaration of the Rights of the Indigenous Peoples, the Convention on the Elimination of All Forms of Discrimination Against Women, the Nairobi Forward Looking Strategies for the

Advancement of Women, Agenda 21 and the Rio Declaration on Environment and Development, the Cairo Declaration, and the Copenhagen Social Summit Declaration. While we agree with most of the provisions of ILO convention 169, we cannot endorse a Convention, which allows national states to remove Indigenous peoples from their lands with military force.

4. We stand in unity behind this '1995 Beijing Declaration of Indigenous Women' which is the fruit of our collective efforts to understand the world and our situation as Indigenous women critique the Draft Platform for Action, and articulate our demands to the international community, the governments, and the NGO's.

5. We, the women of the original peoples of the world have struggled actively to defend our rights to self-determination and to our territories, which have been invaded and colonised by powerful nations and interests. We have been and are continuing to suffer from multiple oppressions; as Indigenous Peoples, as citizens of colonised and neo-colonial countries, as women, and as members of the poorer classes of society. In spite of this, we have been and continue to protect, transmit, and develop our Indigenous Cosmo vision, our science and technologies, our arts and culture, and our Indigenous socio-political economic systems, which are in harmony with the natural laws of mother earth. We still retain the ethical and esthetic values, the knowledge and philosophy, the spirituality, which conserves and nurtures Mother Earth. We are persisting in our struggles for self-determination and for our rights to our territories. This has been shown in our tenacity and capacity to withstand and survive the colonisation happening in our lands in the last 500 years.

6. The 'New World Order" which is engineered by those who have abused and raped Mother Earth, colonised, marginalised, and discriminated against us, is being imposed on us viciously. This is re-colonisation coming under the name of globalisation and trade liberalisation. The forces behind this are the rich industrialised nation-

states, their transnational corporations, financial institutions that they control like the World Bank, the International Monetary Fund, and the World Trade Organisation (WTO). They will cooperate and compete among themselves to the last frontiers of the world's natural resources located on our lands and waters.

7. The Final Agreement of the Uruguay Round of the General Agreement on Tariffs and Trade (GATT) and the establishment of the WTO has created new instruments for the appropriation and privatisation of our community intellectual rights through the introduction of the trade-related intellectual property rights (TRIPS). This facilitates and legitimises the piracy of our biological, cultural and intellectual resources, and heritage by transnational corporations. Our Indigenous values and practice of sharing knowledge among ourselves, and mutual exchange will become things of the past because we are being forced to play by the rules of the market.

8. Bio-prospecting, which is nothing but the alienation of our invaluable intellectual and cultural heritage through scientific collection missions and ethno botanical research, is another feature of re-colonisation. After colonising our lands and appropriating our natural resources, they are now appropriating our human genetic resources, through the Human Genome Diversity Project. Their bid for the patenting of life forms is the ultimate colonisation and co modification of everything we hold sacred. It won't matter anymore that we will disappear because we will be 'immortalised' as 'isolates of historic interest' by the Human Genome Diversity Project.

9. It is an imperative for us, as Indigenous Peoples, to stand in their way, because it means more ethnocide and genocide for us. It will lead to the disappearance of the diverse biological and cultural resources in this world, which we have sustained. It will cause the further erosion and destruction of our Indigenous knowledge, spirituality, and culture. It will exacerbate the conflicts occurring on our lands and communities and our displacement form our ancestral territories.

Critique of the Beijing Draft Platform for Action

10. The Beijing Draft Platform for Action, unfortunately, is not critical at all of the New World Order." It does present a comprehensive list of issues confronting women and an even longer list of actions which governments, the UN and its agencies, multilateral financing institutions, and NGO's should do. It identifies 'the persistent and increasing burden of poverty' as the number one critical concern. It acknowledges that 'most of the goals of the Nairobi Forward Looking Strategies...have not been achieved.' It also acknowledged 'in the past decade the number of women living in poverty has increased disproportionately to the number of men'.

11. However, it does not acknowledge that this poverty is caused by the same powerful nations and interests who have colonised us and are continuing to re-colonise, homogenise, and impose their economic growth development model and monocultures on us. It does not present a coherent analysis of why is it that the goals of 'equality, development, and peace,' become more elusive to women each day in spite of three UN conferences on women since 1975. While it refers to Structural Adjustment Programs (SAPs), it only talks about mitigating its negative impacts, not questioning the basic framework under girding SAPs. It even underscores the importance of trade liberalisation and access to open and dynamic markets, which to us pose the biggest threat to our rights to our territories, resources, intellectual and cultural heritage.

12. The clear bias of the New World Order for big industries, big agri-business corporations, etc., has meant the decimation of traditional livelihood and economic activities of Indigenous peoples like hunting, food gathering and harvesting, reindeer herding, subsistence agriculture, fishing, small handicraft businesses, etc. The non-economic activities of Indigenous women have been ignored and rendered invisible, although these sustain the existence of Indigenous peoples. Our dispossession from our territorial land and water base, upon which our existence and identity depends, must be addressed as a key problem. The Platform is very vague on this.

13. The critical areas of concern it has identified are also critical for Indigenous women. While it correctly identifies unequal access to education and health as areas of concern, it does not question the basic Western orientation of the prevailing education and health systems. It does not reflect the fact that these systems have perpetuated the discrimination against Indigenous peoples. It also does not acknowledge the role of Western media, education, and religion, in eroding the cultural diversity, which exists among Indigenous peoples. These Western systems hasten ethnocide. It does not give proper recognition and importance to Indigenous health care systems and the role of its practitioners.

14. The violence and sexual trafficking of Indigenous women and the increasing numbers of Indigenous women becoming labor exports, has been aggravated by the perpetuation of an economic growth development model which is export-oriented, import-dependent, and mired in foreign debt Military operations conducted on Indigenous peoples lands use rape, sexual-slavery, and sexual trafficking of Indigenous women, to further subjugate Indigenous peoples. The development of tourism to attract foreign capital has also led to the co modification of Indigenous women and the dramatic increase in the incidence of HIV/AIDS. This reality is not addressed by the Platform. Domestic violence and the increasing suicide rates among Indigenous women, especially those who are in highly industrialised countries are caused by psychological alienation and assimilations' policies characteristic of these countries.

15. While it talks about the effects of persecution and armed conflict, it does not acknowledge that many of these armed conflicts are occurring on Indigenous peoples' lands. These armed conflicts are the result of the aggressive actions of transnational corporations and governments to appropriate the remaining resources on Indigenous peoples' territories despite the assertion of

Indigenous peoples to their right to control these resources. It does not recognise that the resolution of armed conflict, especially those happening on Indigenous peoples' lands, lies in the recognition of our rights to self-determination and to our lands and waters. The phrase 'internally displaced' in the text is bracketed, when in fact, this is the reality for many Indigenous peoples all over the world.

16. Its recommended 'strategic objectives' and actions focus on ensuring women's equal access and full participation in decision-making, equal status, equal pay, and integrating and mainstreaming gender perspectives and analysis. These objectives are hollow and meaningless if the inequality between nations, races, classes, and genders, are not challenged at the same time. Equal pay and equal status in the so-called First World is made possible because of the perpetuation of a development model which is not only non-sustainable but causes the increasing violation of the human rights of women, Indigenous peoples, and nations elsewhere. The Platform's over-emphasis of gender discrimination and gender equality de-politicises the issues confronting Indigenous women.

Indigenous Women's Proposals and Demands

17. Within the context of our understanding of our situation and our critique of the 'New World Order' and of the Beijing Draft Platform for Action, we present the following demands.

18. That all governments and international non-governmental and governmental organisations recognise the right of Indigenous peoples to self-determination, and enshrine the historical, political, social, cultural, economic, and religious rights of the Indigenous peoples in their constitutions and legal systems.

Recognise And Respect Our Rights to Self Determination

19. That the governments amend the ILO Convention 169 to remove the section, which allows nations states to remove Indigenous peoples from their lands through military force, and thereafter ratify and implement it.

20. That the 1994 Final Draft Declaration on the Rights of Indigenous peoples be adopted and ratified by governments without any revisions and reservations. That the full participation of Indigenous peoples in the open-ended working group of the Commission of Human Rights to further elaborate on the draft will be ensured.

21. That the 's' in term Indigenous 'peoples' be put in all United Nations documents, declarations, and conventions. That, hereafter, we will not be referred to as ethnic minorities or cultural communities but as Indigenous peoples.[1]

Recognise and Respect Our Right to Our Territories, and Right to Development, Education and Health

22. We demand that the international community and governments recognise and respect our rights to our territories. This includes our right to decide what to do with our lands and territories and to develop in an integrated, sustainable way, according to our own Cosmo vision.

23. We urge the governments who are opening up our territories to foreign investors especially to mining corporations, to respect these rights. Full disclosure of development projects and investments to be put into our territories should be done. We should be fully involved in making decisions on these matters. The corporations or the governments, which allowed this devastation, should rehabilitate indigenous peoples' lands which have been ravaged by mining corporations, or which have become dumping sites of toxic, radioactive and hazardous wastes.

24. That the governments, international organisations and NGO's assume their responsibility to alter their policies and allocate resources for the inter-cultural and bilingual educational system, and the development of Indigenous health care systems according to our cultural principles and Cosmo vision. That book, audio and video materials, etc. be screened and purged of discriminatory, racist, and sexist content.

25. That the governments implement realistic policies which will solve the problem of illiteracy among Indigenous and peasant women, providing them access to intercultural and bilingual education which respects Indigenous cosmologies, promotes non-sexist formative education which puts women and men in touch with the land.

26. That the governments and international community implement health policies which guarantee accessible, appropriate, affordable, and quality services for Indigenous peoples and which respect and promote the reproductive health of Indigenous women. That budget allocations to health and other social services be increased to at least twenty percent of the national budget and that a significant amount of this goes to Indigenous people's communities.

27. That the Indigenous health care systems and practices of Indigenous peoples are accorded the proper recognition and respect and the roles of Indigenous health practitioners and healers be further enhanced.

28. That the dumping of hazardous drugs, chemicals, and contraceptives on Indigenous peoples communities be stopped. We demand that coercive family planning services, like mass sterilisation of Indigenous women and coercive abortion programs be stopped. Those population policies like transmigration be condemned and halted.

29. We demand that uranium mining taking place in our lands and nuclear testing in our territories and waters be stopped. If no uranium mining is done then there will be no nuclear weapons, nuclear reactors, and nuclear accidents.

Stop Human Rights Violations and Violence Against Indigenous Women

30. That the United Nations creates the necessary mechanisms to monitor the Indigenous peoples situation especially those facing the threat of extinction and human rights violations and to stop these ethnocide and genocidal practices.

31. Call on all the Media and Communication Systems to realise that Indigenous women refuse to continue to be treated and considered as exotic, decorative, sexual objects, or study-objects, but instead to be recognised as human beings with their own thinking and feeling capabilities and abilities for personal development; spiritually, intellectually, and materially.

32. Demand for an investigation of the reported cases of sexual slavery and the rape of Indigenous women by the military men happening in areas of armed conflict, such as those within Karen territories in Burma, Chittagong Hill Tracts in Bangladesh, etc. The perpetrators should be persecuted and the survivors are provided justice and rehabilitation and services.

33. Demand for an investigation of the forcible mass sterilisation and anti-fertility programs done among Indigenous women. Identify which international and national agencies are responsible for these and make them accountable.

34. That all acts of discrimination against Indigenous Women be considered and punished as a crime.

35. That the governments create juridical and social instruments adequate to protect women from domestic and state violence.

36. That Indigenous customary laws and justice systems, which are supportive of women victims of violence, be recognised and reinforced. That Indigenous laws, customs, and traditions which are discriminatory to women be eradicated.

37. That all internally displaced Indigenous peoples are allowed to return to their own communities, and the necessary rehabilitation and support services are provided to them.

Recognise and Respect Our Rights to Our Intellectual and Cultural Heritage; Our Rights to Control the Biological Diversity in Our Territories

38. We demand that our inalienable rights to our intellectual and cultural heritage be recognised and respected. We

will resist all processes seeking to destroy this heritage and alienate our resources and knowledge from us.

39. We demand that the western concept and practice of intellectual property rights as defined by TRIPS in GATT, not be applied to Indigenous peoples communities and territories. We demand that the World Trade Organisation recognise our intellectual and cultural rights and not allow the domain of private intellectual rights and corporate monopolies to violate these.

40. We call for a stop to the patenting of all life forms. This to us is the ultimate co modification of life, which we hold sacred.

41. We demand that the Human Genome Diversity Project be condemned and stopped. Those responsible for this project should be asked to make an accounting of all the genetic collections they have taken from Indigenous peoples and have these returned to the owners of these genes. The applications for patents to these genetic materials should be stopped and no applications, thereafter, should be accepted and processed. Indigenous peoples should be invited to participate in the ongoing discussions in UNESCO on the bioethics of the Human Genome.

42. We demand that governments at the local, regional, and national levels recognise our intellectual community rights and support us in our defense of these rights, an obligation that they have undertaken as Parties to the Biodiversity Convention.

43. We will continue to freely use our biodiversity for meeting our local needs, while ensuring that the biodiversity base of our local economies will not be eroded. We will revitalise and rejuvenate our biological and cultural heritage and continue to be the guardians and custodians of our knowledge and biodiversity.

Ensure Political Participation of Indigenous Women And Enhance Their Capabilities and Access to Resources

44. We demand equal political participation in the Indigenous and modern structures of socio-political structures and systems at all levels.

45. We will dialogue with non-indigenous women's organisations and formations to implement a realistic plan of solidarity with us.

46. We ask that NGOs that work with Indigenous women be guided by principles of mutual respect and promote the full participation of Indigenous women in action and in articulating issues regarding Indigenous women and indigenous peoples.

47. Call on the funding agencies and donor agencies that support and promote women's organisations and programs, to share space and financial resources in order to promote the development of Indigenous women.

48. We will work towards reinforcing our own organisations, enhancing communications between us, and gain the space that is rightfully ours, as members of specific identities (nations and cultures) within the Decade of Indigenous peoples and other institutions that represent governmental and non-governmental organisations.

49. We will work towards the holding of an International Conference of Indigenous Women, which will be held as part of the celebration of the International Decade of the World's indigenous peoples.

50. We give our sincere thanks to the Chinese Organising Committee and the Chinese people for their efforts in hosting and providing hospitality to us.

Approved and Signed on 7 September 1995 at The Indigenous Women's Tent, Huairou, Beijing, China.

Source: http://www.ipcb.org/resolutions/htmls/dec_beijing.html

Notes

1. The evolution in terminologies also indicates the struggle for self-determination. From being called ethnic minorities or cultural communities to indigenous peoples is the path that the indigenous peoples have taken over the years. This further establishes the fact that indigenous peoples are the original settlers and not minorities among the majorities.

4

No to Patenting of Life

Indigenous Peoples' Statement on the Trade-Related Aspects of Intellectual Property Rights (TRIPS) of the WTO Agreement

We, Indigenous Peoples from around the world, believe that nobody can own what exists in nature except nature herself. A human being cannot own its own mother. Humankind is part of Mother Nature, we have created nothing and we can in no way claim to be owners of what does not belong to us. But time and again, western legal property regimes have been imposed on us, contradicting our own cosmologies and values.

We View with regret and anxiety how, Article 27.3b of the Trade-Related Aspects of Intellectual Property Rights (TRIPS) of the World Trade Organisation (WTO) Agreements will further denigrate and undermine our rights to our cultural and intellectual heritage, our plant, animal, and even human genetic resources and discriminate against our indigenous ways of thinking and behaving. This Article makes an artificial distinction between plants, animals, and micro-organisms and between 'essentially biological' and 'microbiological processes' for making plants and animals. As far as we are concerned all these are life forms and life creating processes which are sacred and which should not become the subject of proprietary ownership.

We know that intellectual property rights as defined in the TRIPS Agreement are monopoly rights given to individuals or legal persons (e.g. transnational corporations) who can prove that the inventions or innovations they made are novel, involve an innovative step and are capable of industrial application. The application of this form of property rights over living things as if they are mechanical or industrial inventions is inappropriate.

Indigenous knowledge and cultural heritage are collectively and accretionally evolved through generations. Thus, no single person can claim invention or discovery of medicinal plants, seeds or other living things.

The inherent conflict between these two knowledge systems and the manner in which they are protected and used will cause further disintegration of our communal values and practices. It can also lead to infighting between indigenous communities over who has ownership over a particular knowledge or innovation. Furthermore, it goes against the very essence of indigenous spirituality which regards all creation as sacred.

We are aware of the various implications of the TRIPS Agreement on our lives as indigenous peoples. It will lead to the appropriation of our traditional medicinal plants and seeds and our indigenous knowledge on health, agriculture and biodiversity conservation. It will undermine food security, since the diversity and agricultural production on which our communities depend would be eroded and would be controlled by individual, private and foreign interests. In addition, the TRIPS Agreement will substantially weaken our access to and control over genetic and biological resources; plunder our resources and territories; and contribute to the deterioration of our quality of life.

In the review of the Article 27.3 (b) of the TRIPS Agreement, therefore, our proposals are as follows:

This Article should be amended to categorically disallow the patenting of life forms. Thus, the revised Article 27.3b should clearly prohibit the patenting of plants and animals including all their parts, meaning, genes, gene sequences, cells, proteins, seeds, etc. It should also prohibit the patenting of natural processes involving the use of plants, animals and other living organisms and their parts and processes used in producing variations of plants, animals, and micro-organisms.

The provision for the protection of plant varieties by a patent, a *sui generis* system, or a combination of both should be amended and elaborated further: It should:

Disallow the use of patents to protect plant varieties.

Ensure that the *sui generis* system which may be created will protect the knowledge and innovations and practices in farming, agriculture, health and medical care, and conservation of biodiversity of indigenous peoples and farmers.

Build upon the indigenous methods and customary laws protecting knowledge and heritage and biological resources.

Ensure that the protection offered to the indigenous and traditional innovation, knowledge, and practices are consistent with the Convention of Biological Diversity (i.e. Articles 8j, 10c, 17.2, and 18.4) and the International Undertaking on Plant Genetic Resources.

Allow for the right of indigenous peoples and farmers to continue their traditional practices of saving, sharing, and exchanging seeds; and harvesting, cultivating, and using medicinal plants.

Prevent the appropriation, theft, and piracy of indigenous seeds, medicinal plants, and the knowledge around the use of these by researchers, academic institutions, and corporations, etc.

Integrate the principle and practice of prior informed consent, which means that the consent of indigenous peoples' as communities or as collectivities should be obtained before any research or collection of plants will be undertaken. The right of indigenous peoples to veto any bioprospecting activity should be guaranteed. Mechanisms to enforce prior informed consent should be installed.

Prevent the destruction and conversion of indigenous peoples' lands which are rich in biodiversity through projects like mines, monocrop commercial plantations, dams, etc. and recognise the rights of indigenous peoples to these lands and territories.

We urge the WTO Member-States to put the amendment of the TRIPS Agreement as a priority item in agenda of the forthcoming WTO Ministerial Conference in Seattle. The implementation of the TRIPS Agreement in its present form will have devastating social and environmental consequences which will be irreversible. It is an imperative, therefore, that this Agreement be amended to prohibit the patenting of lifeforms and the piracy of indigenous peoples knowledge and resources.

We also call on all the WTO Member-States to work for the extension of the deadline of the implementation of Article 27.3b of TRIPS to the year 2006, five years after the completion of the review of this has been done.

Finally, we reiterate our commitment to sustain our struggle to have our rights to our intellectual and cultural heritage and our lands and resources promoted and protected. We call on WTO to become an instrument in promoting our rights instead of enacting and imposing Agreements which are violative or undermining our rights as distinct peoples.

Signed at the United Nations, Geneva, Switzerland, on 25 July 1999.

Signatories:

Indigenous Peoples' Organisations, NGOs and Networks

5

Indigenous Peoples' Seattle Declaration

On the occasion of the Third Ministerial Meeting of the World Trade Organisation, 30th November to 3rd December 1999.

We, the Indigenous Peoples from various regions of the world, have come to Seattle to express our great concern over how WTO is destroying Mother Earth and the cultural and biological diversity of which we are a part.

Trade liberalisation and export-oriented development, which are the overriding principles and policies pushed by WTO, are creating the most adverse impacts on the lives of Indigenous Peoples. Our inherent right to self-determination, our sovereignty as nations, and treaties and other constructive agreements which Indigenous nations and peoples have negotiated with other nation-states, are undermined by most of WTO Agreements. The disproportionate impact of these Agreements on our communities, whether through environmental degradation or the militarisation and violence that often accompanies development projects, is serious and therefore should be addressed immediately.

The WTO Agreement on Agriculture (AOA), which promotes export competition and import liberalisation, has allowed the entry of cheap agricultural products into our communities. It is causing the destruction of ecologically rational and sustainable agricultural practices of Indigenous Peoples.

Food security and the production of traditional food crops have been seriously compromised. Incidents of diabetes, cancers, and hypertension have significantly increased among Indigenous Peoples because of the scarcity of traditional foods and the dumping of junk food into our communities.

Small-scale farm production is giving way to commercial cash-crop plantations further concentrating ancestral lands into the hands of few agri-corporations and landlords. This has led to the dislocation of scores of people from our communities who then migrate to nearby cities and become the urban homeless and jobless.

The WTO Forests Products Agreement promotes free trade in forest products. By eliminating developed country tariffs on wood products by the year 2000, and developing country tariffs by 2003, the Agreement will result in the deforestation of many of the world's ecosystems in which Indigenous Peoples live.

Mining laws in many countries are being changed to allow free entry of foreign mining corporations, to enable them to buy and own mineral lands, and to freely displace Indigenous Peoples from their ancestral territories. These large-scale commercial mining and oil extraction activities continue to degrade our lands and fragile ecosystems, and pollute the soil, water, and air in our communities.

The appropriation of our lands and resources and the aggressive promotion of consumerist and individualistic Western culture continue to destroy traditional lifestyles and cultures. The result is environmental degradation but also ill health, alienation, and high levels of stress manifested in high rates of alcoholism and suicides.

The theft and patenting of our biogenetic resources is facilitated by TRIPs of WTO. Some plants which Indigenous Peoples have discovered, cultivated, and used for food, medicine, and for sacred rituals are already patented in the U.S., Japan, and Europe. A few examples of these are ayahuasca, quinoa, and sangre de drago in forests of South America; kava in the Pacific, and turmeric and bitter melon in Asia. The TRIPs Agreement threatens our access and control over our biological diversity and control over our traditional knowledge and intellectual heritage.

Article 27.3b of TRIPs Agreement allows the patenting of life forms and makes an artificial distinction between plants, animals, and microorganisms. The distinction between 'essentially biological' and 'non-biological' and 'microbiological' processes is also erroneous. As far as we are concerned all these are life forms and life-creating processes which are sacred and which should not become the subject of private property ownership.

Finally, the liberalisation of investments and the service sectors, which is pushed by the General Agreement of Services (GATS), reinforces the domination and monopoly control of foreign corporations over strategic parts of the economy. The World Bank and the International Monetary Fund impose conditionality of liberalisation, deregulation and privatisation on countries caught in the debt trap. This conditionality is reinforced further by WTO.

In light of the adverse impacts and consequences of WTO Agreements identified above, we, Indigenous Peoples present the following demands:

We urgently call for a social and environmental justice analysis, which will look into the Agreements' cumulative effects on Indigenous Peoples. Indigenous Peoples should be equal participants in establishing the criteria and indicators for these analyses so that they take into consideration spiritual as well as cultural aspects.

A review of the Agreements should be done to address all of the inequities and imbalances, which adversely affect Indigenous Peoples. The proposals to address some of these are as follows;

For the Agreement on Agriculture

(a) It should not include in its coverage small-scale farmers who are mainly engaged in production for domestic use and sale in the local markets.

(b) It should ensure the recognition and protection of rights of Indigenous Peoples to their territories and their resources, as well as their rights to continue practicing their indigenous sustainable agriculture and resource management practices and traditional livelihoods.

(c) It should ensure the food security and the capacity of Indigenous Peoples to produce, consume and trade their traditional foods.

With regard to the liberalisation of services and investments, we recommend the following:

(a) It must stop unsustainable mining, commercial planting of monocrops, dam construction, oil exploration, land conversion to golf clubs, logging, and other activities which destroy Indigenous Peoples' lands and violate the rights of indigenous peoples' to their territories and resources.

(b) The right of Indigenous Peoples to their traditional lifestyles, cultural norms and values should likewise be recognised and protected.

(c) The liberalisation of services, especially in the areas of health, should not be allowed if it will prevent Indigenous Peoples from having access to free, culturally appropriate as well as quality health services.

(d) The liberalisation of finance services, which makes the world a global casino, should be regulated.

On TRIPs Agreement, the proposals are as follows:

(a) Article 27.3b should be amended to categorically disallow the patenting of life forms. It should clearly prohibit the patenting of micro-organisms, plants, animals, including all their parts, whether they are genes, gene sequences, cells, cell lines, proteins, or seeds.

(b) It should also prohibit the patenting of natural processes, whether these are biological or microbiological, involving the use of plants, animals and microorganisms and their parts in producing variations of plants, animals and microorganisms.

(c) It should ensure the exploration and development of alternative forms of protection outside of the dominant western intellectual property rights regime. Such alternatives must protect the knowledge and innovations and practices in agriculture, health care, and conservation of biodiversity, and should build upon indigenous methods and customary laws protecting knowledge, heritage and biological resources.

(d) It should ensure that the protection offered to indigenous and traditional knowledge, innovation and practices is consistent with the Convention on Biological Diversity (i.e., Articles 8j, 10c, 17.2, and 18.4) and the International Undertaking on Plant Genetic Resources.

(e) It should allow for the right of Indigenous Peoples and farmers to continue their traditional practices of saving, sharing and exchanging seeds, and cultivating, harvesting and using medicinal plants.

(f) It should prohibit scientific researchers and corporations from appropriating and patenting indigenous seeds, medicinal plants, and related knowledge about these life forms. The principles of prior informed consent and right of veto by Indigenous Peoples should be respected.

If the earlier proposals cannot be ensured, we call for the removal of the Agreement on Agriculture, the Forest Products Agreements and the TRIPs Agreement from the WTO.

We call on the member-states of the WTO not to allow for another round whilst the review and rectification of the implementation of existing agreements has not been done. We reject the proposals for an investment treaty, competition, accelerated industrial tariffs, government procurement, and the creation of a working group on biotechnology.

We urge the WTO to reform itself to become democratic, transparent and accountable. If it fails to do this, we call for the abolition of the WTO.

We urge the member nation-states of the WTO to endorse the adoption by the UN General Assembly of the current text of the UN Declaration on the Rights of Indigenous Peoples and the ratification of ILO Convention 169.

We call on the peoples' organisations and NGOs to support this 'Indigenous Peoples' Seattle Declaration' and to promote it among their members.

We believe that the whole philosophy underpinning the WTO Agreements and the principles and policies it promotes contradict our core values, spirituality and worldviews, as well as our concepts and practices of development, trade and environmental protection. Therefore, we challenge the WTO to redefine its principles and practices toward a [sustainable communities] paradigm, and to recognise and allow for the continuation of other worldviews and models of development.

Indigenous peoples, undoubtedly, are the ones most adversely affected by globalisation and by the WTO Agreements. However, we believe that it is also us who can offer viable alternatives to the dominant economic growth, export-oriented development model. Our sustainable lifestyles and cultures, traditional knowledge, cosmologies, spirituality, values of collectivity, reciprocity, respect and reverence for Mother Earth, are crucial in the search for a transformed society where justice, equity, and sustainability will prevail.

Statement by the Indigenous Peoples' Caucus convened and sponsored by the Indigenous Environmental Network USA/CANADA, Seventh Generation Fund USA, International Indian Treaty Council, Indigenous Peoples Council on Bio colonialism, the Abya Yala Fund, and TEBTEBBA (Indigenous Peoples' International Centre for Policy Research and Education), 1 December 1999, Seattle, Washington, USA.

Indigenous Peoples' Organisations participating in the Seattle WTO that signed on to this Declaration are listed below:

- Nilo Cayuqueo, Abya Yala Fund, USA
- Victoria Tauli-Corpuz, Indigenous Peoples Network for Policy Research and Education, Philippines
- Tom Goldtooth, Indigenous Environmental Network, USA/Canada
- Antonio Gonzales, International Indian Treaty Council, International
- Margarita Gutierrez, Social Commission for The Development of The Nanhu, Mexico
- Debra Harry, Indigenous Peoples Council on Biocolonialism, USA

- Clemencia Herrera Nemarayema, National Indigena Organisation of Colombia, South America
- Chief Johnny Jackson, Klickitat Band of Yakama, Elder Committee of Indigenous Environmental Network, USA/ Canada
- Carol Kalafatic, International Indian Treaty Council, International
- Dune Lankard, Eyak Alaska Preservation Council, USA
- Chief Arthur Manual, Interior Alliance of First Nations, Canada
- Alvin Manitopyes, Cree Strong Heart Environmental and Wellness Society, Canada
- Jim Main Sr., Gros Ventre White Clay Society, USA
- Jose Matos, Indigenous Alliance Without Borders, USA/ Mexico
- Esther Nahgahnub, Anishinabeg Treaty 1854 Committee, USA
- Chris Peters, Seventh Generation Fund, USA
- Priscilla Settee, Indigenous Women's Network, USA/ Canada
- Taita Stanley, Movimiento de la Juventad Kuna, Panama
- Chaz Wheelock, Great Lakes Regional Indigenous Environmental Network, USA/Canada
- Clemente Ibe Wilson, Movimiento de la Juventad Kuna, Panama

6

Declaration of the First International Forum of Indigenous Peoples in Climate Change

Lyon, France 4-6 September 2000

Introduction

We, the Indigenous Peoples, have historically played an active role in the conservation of eco-systems crucial to the prevention of climate change such as forests, wetlands and coastal and marine areas. Long ago, our sciences foretold of the severe impacts of Western 'development' models based on indiscriminate clear-cutting, oil exploitation, mining, carbon-emitting industries, permanent organic pollutants and the insatiable consumption of the industrialised countries. Today, these unsustainable models threaten the very life of Mother Earth and the lives of all of us who are her children.

The scientists of Western society have dismissed us as sentimental and superstitious and accused us of being an obstacle to development. Paradoxically, those that previously turned deaf ears to our warnings, now are dismayed because their own model of 'development' endangers our Mother Earth.

At long last, the international community has been forced to recognise that climate change threatens the very survival of humanity. Despite the recognition of our role in preventing global warming, when it comes time to sign international conventions like the United Nations Framework Convention on Climate Change, once again, our right to participate in national and international discussions that directly affect our Peoples and territories is denied.

Our active opposition to oil exploration, logging and mining helps prevent the accelerated deterioration of the climate. Nonetheless, our territories have been handed over to national and multinational corporations, which exploit our natural resources in an indiscriminate and unsustainable fashion.

Any decision or action that the Conference of Parties of the United Nations Framework Convention on Climate Change (UNFCCC) or recommendations to other organs must include our full and effective participation. Our efforts to maintain the integrity of Mother Earth have been recognised by the United Nations and our participation includes and is established by:

> The Working Group on Indigenous Populations under the Sub commission of Prevention of Discrimination and the Protection of Minorities of the UN.
>
> The Working Group on Article 8 (j) and Convex Articles of the Convention on Biological Diversity which includes, among other issues, systems of traditional knowledge; the recognition of traditional knowledge systems in the Intergovernmental Dialogue on Forests (including the Panel, Intergovernmental Forum and the United Nations Forum on Forests).

The Permanent Forum on Indigenous Affairs to be established by ECOSOC in the United Nations; the recognition of the Indigenous as Major Groups in Agenda 21, chapter 26, and the Rio Declaration; ILO Convention 169 on Indigenous and Tribal Peoples in independent countries; the elaboration of policies of the European Union, the United Nations Development Programme (UNDP) and the World Bank guidelines on Indigenous Peoples.

Before the signing of the Kyoto Protocol, we had already made concrete political contributions to mitigating climate change. For example, Indigenous Peoples of the Amazon forged a mutually beneficial alliance with European Cities in joint program of the Climate Alliance, the Coordinator of Indigenous Organisations of the Amazon Basin (COICA) and the

International Alliance of Indigenous and Tribal Peoples of the Tropical Forests.

Key positions of Indigenous Peoples present at the UNFCCC 13th Session of Subsidiary Bodies Meeting are as follows:

SINKS

Our intrinsic relation with Mother Earth obliges us to oppose the inclusion of sinks in the Clean Development Mechanism (CDM) because it reduces our sacred land and territories to mere carbon sequestration which is contrary to our Cosmo vision and philosophy of life. Sinks in the CDM would constitute a worldwide strategy for expropriating our lands and territories and violating our fundamental rights that would culminate in a new form of colonialism. Sinks in the CDM would not help to reduce GHG emissions; rather it would provide industrialised countries with a ploy to avoid reducing their emissions at source.

Clean Development Mechanism: The Clean Development Mechanism (CDM) established by the Kyoto Protocol offers both negative and positive possibilities. The CDM will not be a solution to global warming if it diffuses or obfuscates the responsibility of industrialised countries to reduce their GHG. It must not be used to allow Annex I countries to continue poisoning the environment. Sinks in the CDM pose the threat of invasion and lose of our land and territories by establishing new regimes for protected areas and privatisation. We emphatically oppose the inclusion of sinks, plantations, nuclear power, mega hydroelectric and coal. Furthermore, we oppose the development of a carbon market that would broaden the scope of globalisation. However, we do support the Positive List including the development of alternative energies that foster sustainable development.

Public Participation: Indigenous Peoples demand that the principles of transparency, prior informed consultation and consent, independent third party verification and monitoring, benefit sharing, risk reduction, appeals mechanism and compensation be guaranteed. Furthermore, we emphasise the need for these principles to be applied in culturally and linguistically appropriate manners.

LULUCF

Land use change and forestry (LULUCF) in the Protocol have profound consequences for our lands and territories since it does not recognise the land rights nor customary land use of Indigenous Peoples.

The definitions of afforestation, reforestation and deforestation must not contribute to the destruction of our native eco-systems, forests, lands, and territories or to the violation of our collective and individual rights.

A broad definition of 'additional activities' would permit Annex I countries to meet the most of their emissions reduction targets with LULUCF and continue with 'business as usual' which would not mitigate climate change at all. We reject granting carbon credits for 'additional activities'.

Adaptation Fund

We enthusiastically support the creation and funding of the Adaptation Fund. Since we sadly foresee that our peoples will continue to suffer the adverse impacts of climate change, we demand our inclusion as beneficiaries of such a Fund. Monies for this Fund should be garnered from punitive fines for the failure of Annex I countries to meet their emissions reduction targets or for inaccurate carbon accounting or national inventories.

AIJ Pilot Phase

We deem it necessary that the UNFCCC support the need of Indigenous Peoples to conduct our own independent critique and evaluation of AIJ projects and their impacts and ramifications for the rights and lands of our peoples.

Articles 5, 7 & 8

We propose that our Peoples and experts be included in the assessment and analysis of climate change in Annex I countries provided for in Articles 5, 7 & 8.

Capacity Building

Since our peoples are on the frontlines of the adverse impacts of climate change, we must be included in the UNFCCC capacity building initiatives and propose that special, specific capacity building be undertaken for Indigenous Peoples. Such capacity building would fortify our ability to exercise our right to full participation in the climate change negotiations.

Compliance

We call for the cancellation of carbon credits and punitive fines if Annex I countries fail to meet their emission reduction targets or submit inaccurate Carbon accounting or inventories.

Given these considerations, we recommend:

1. That the Conference of Parties VI recognise the fundamental role of Indigenous Peoples and their organisations in climate change prevention and environmental conservation and accredit Indigenous Peoples with special status in all the organs, activities and COPs of the UNFCCC.
2. That COP 6 approves the creation of a Working Group of Indigenous Peoples on Climate Change, as well as, recognising the Forum of Indigenous People on Climate Change. Furthermore, that COP 6 provide the necessary support including full effective participation in all levels of discussion, decision-making and implementation, as well as ensuring that the necessary funding be provided to guarantee said participation and to strengthen its capacity.
3. That the UNFCCC and its processes establish relations with other spaces and processes that affect Indigenous Peoples, including the Commission on Human Rights, ECOSOC, the pending Permanent Forum of Indigenous Peoples, ILO, the Convention on Biodiversity and the Inter-governmental Forum on Forests among others.
4. That the UNFCCC and its Secretariat create, provide and distribute information on the negotiations and process for Indigenous Peoples to further foster our participation, positions adoption and contributions.
5. That the decisions on the implementation of the Kyoto Protocol include provisions that recognise and establish all the fundamental rights of Indigenous Peoples.
6. That the Subsidiary Bodies recommend that COP 6 refrain from adopting guidelines for the CDM until substantial

debate and discussions including Indigenous Peoples occurs.

We, the Indigenous Peoples, consider that the concerns and recommendations expressed in this declaration will help the peoples of the world to reduce climate change and contribute to sustainable development.

Signed by the following Indigenous Peoples and local community representatives present at the United Nations Framework Convention on Climate Change Subsidiary Bodies meetings in Lyon, France, 8 September 2000:

Parshu Ram Tamang, Nepal. International Alliance of Indigenous and Tribal Peoples of the Tropical Forests
Alejandro Argumedo, Peru, Indigenous Knowledge Program

Mario Ibarra, Geneva. International Indian Treaty Council

Clark Peteru, Samoa. Indigenous Peoples' Biodiversity Network

Hector Huertas, Panama. Meso American Indigenous Organisations on Climate Change

Kalimba Zephyrin, Rwanda, Association for the Promotion of Batwans

Edwin Vasquez, Peru. Inter-ethnic Development Association of the Peruvian Jungle (AIDESEP)

Johnson Cerda, Ecuador. Amazon Alliance

Antonio Jacanamijoy, Columbia. Coordinating Body of the Indigenous Organisations of the Amazon Basin (COICA)

Jose Luis Gonzalez, Venezuela. The Indigenous Federation of Bolivar

Hendro Sangkoyo, Indonesia. Consortium for Community Forest Systems

Raymond de Chavez, Philippines. TEBTEBBA Foundation, Indigenous Peoples International Center for Policy, Research and Education

Sam Ferrer, Philippines. Climate Action Network

7

The Kimberley Declaration

International Indigenous Peoples Summit on Sustainable Development Khoi San Territory

Kimberley, South Africa, 20-23 August 2002

We, the Indigenous Peoples, walk to the future in the footprints of our ancestors (Kari Oca Declaration, Brazil, 30 May 1992)

We the Indigenous Peoples of the World assembled here reaffirm the Kari Oca Declaration and the Indigenous Peoples' Earth Charter. We again reaffirm our previous declarations on human and environmental sustainability.[1]

Since 1992, the ecosystems of the earth have been compounding in charge. We are in crisis. We are in an accelerating spiral of climate change that will not abide unsustainable greed.

Today we reaffirm our relationship to Mother Earth and our responsibility to coming generations to uphold peace, equity and justice. We continue to pursue the commitments made at Earth Summit as reflected in this political declaration and the accompanying plan of action. The commitments, which, were made to Indigenous Peoples in Agenda 21, including our full and effective participation, have not been implemented due to the lack of political will.

As peoples, we reaffirm our rights to self-determination and to own, control and manage our ancestral lands and territories, waters and other resources. Our lands and territories are at the core of our existence – we are the land

and the land is us, we have a distinct spiritual and material relationship with our lands and territories, and they are inextricably linked to our survival and to the preservation and further development of our knowledge systems and cultures, conservation and sustainable use of biodiversity and ecosystem management.

We have the right to determine and establish priorities and strategies for our self -development and for the use of our lands, territories and other resources. We demand that free, prior and informed consent must be the principle of approving or rejecting any project or activity affecting our lands, territories and other resources.

We are the original peoples tied to the land by our umbilical cords and the dust of our ancestors. Our special places are sacred and demand the highest respect. Disturbing the remains of our families and elders is desecration of the greatest magnitude and constitutes a grave violation of our human rights. We call for the full and immediate repatriation of all Khoi San human remains currently held in museums and other institutions throughout the world, as well as all the human remains of all other Indigenous Peoples. We maintain the rights to our sacred and ceremonial sites and ancestral remains, including access to burial, archaeological and historic sites.

The national, regional and international acceptance and recognition of Indigenous Peoples is central to the achievement of human and environmental sustainability. Our traditional knowledge systems must be respected, promoted and protected; our collective intellectual property rights must be guaranteed and ensured. Our traditional knowledge is not in the public domain; it is collective, cultural and intellectual property protected under our customary law. Unauthorised use and misappropriation of traditional knowledge is theft.

Economic globalisation constitutes one of the main obstacles for the recognition of the rights of Indigenous Peoples. Transnational corporations and industrialised countries impose their global agenda on the negotiations and agreements of the United Nations system, the World Bank, the International Monetary Fund, the World Trade Organisation and other bodies which reduce the rights enshrined in national constitutions and in international conventions and agreements. Unsustainable extraction, harvesting, production and consumption patterns lead to climate change, widespread pollution and environmental destruction, evicting us from our lands and creating immense levels of poverty and disease.

We are deeply concerned that the activities of multinational mining corporations on Indigenous lands have led to the loss and desecration of our lands, as exemplified here on Khoi San territory. These activities have caused immense health problems, interfered with access to, and occupation of our sacred sites, destroyed and depleted Mother Earth, and undermined our cultures.

Indigenous Peoples, our lands and territories are not objects of tourism development. We have rights and responsibilities towards our lands and territories. We are responsible to defend our lands, territories and indigenous peoples against tourism exploitation by governments, development agencies, private enterprises, NGOs, and individuals.

Recognising the vital role that pastoralism and hunting gathering play in the livelihoods of many Indigenous Peoples, we urge governments to recognise, accept, support and invest in pastoralism and hunting gathering as viable and sustainable economic systems.

We reaffirm the rights of our peoples, nations and communities, our women, men, elders and youth to physical, mental, social, and spiritual well being.

We are determined to ensure the equal participation of all Indigenous Peoples throughout the world in all aspects of planning for a sustainable future with the inclusion of women, men, elders and youth. Equal access to resources is required to achieve this participation.

We urge the United Nations to promote respect for the recognition, observance and enforcement of treaties, agreements and other constructive arrangements concluded between Indigenous Peoples and states, or their successors, according to their original spirit and intent, and to have the states honour and respect such treaties, agreements and other constructive arrangements.

Language is the voice of our ancestors from the beginning of time. The preservation, securing and development of our languages are a matter of extreme urgency language is part of the soul of our nations, our being and the pathway to the future.

In case of the establishment of partnerships in order to achieve human and environmental sustainability, these partnerships must be established according to the following principles: our rights to the land and to self determination, honesty, transparency and good faith; free, prior and informed consent; respect and recognition of our cultures, languages and spiritual beliefs.

We welcome the establishment of the United Nations Permanent Forum on Indigenous Issues and urge the UN to secure all the necessary political, institutional and financial support so that it can function effectively according to its mandate as contained in ECOSOC Resolution E/2000/22. We support the continuation of the United Nations Working Group on Indigenous Populations based on the importance of its mandate to set international standards on the rights of Indigenous Peoples.

We call for a World Conference on Indigenous Peoples and Sustainable Development as a culmination of the United Nations International Decade for the World's Indigenous Peoples (1995-2004) and as a concrete follow up to the World Summit on Sustainable Development.

We continue to meet in the spirit of unity inspired by the Khoi San people and their hospitality. We reaffirm our mutual solidarity as Indigenous Peoples of the world in our struggle for social and environmental justice.

Note

1. Including the Draft Declaration on the Rights of Indigenous Peoples; the Charter of the International Alliance of Indigenous and Tribal Peoples of the Tropical Forests; the Mataatua Declaration; the Santa Cruz Declaration on Intellectual Property; the Leticia Declaration of Indigenous Peoples and Other Forest Dependent Peoples on the Sustainable Use and Management of All Types of Forests; the Charter of Indigenous Peoples of the Arctic and the Far East Siberia; the Bali Indigenous Peoples Political Declaration; and, the Declaration of the Indigenous Peoples of Eastern Africa in the Regional WSSD Preparatory Meeting.

8

Indigenous Delegates' Statement to the World Bank[1] at the Indigenous Peoples Roundtable

17-18 October 2002

Final Indigenous Declaration

Reaffirming that indigenous peoples do not accept the World Bank's March 2001 revised Draft Indigenous Peoples' Policy (OP/BP4.10) as an effective instrument for safeguarding the rights and interests of indigenous peoples affected by its development projects and programmes;

Recalling that we as indigenous peoples consider that we have so far been denied the opportunity to significantly shape the outcome of the policy revision and that the Bank has not addressed our principal concerns and our proposals on how to improve the existing policy;

Stressing that, as it stands, we as indigenous peoples do not feel empowered by Draft OP/BP 4.10 because our rights are not recognised and for this reason, we reject this draft revised policy because it does not respect our rights guaranteed under international law;

Emphasising that the Bank's mission of poverty reduction and sustainable development cannot be achieved without respecting and recognising our fundamental rights as indigenous peoples;

Reiterating that the World Bank has a duty to respect international human rights law and should ensure that the standards it sets in its guidelines for its loan operations are consistent with its obligations under such law;

We, the undersigned representatives and members of indigenous peoples' organisations and indigenous experts who have come from different regions of the world to participate in a roundtable discussion with the World Bank regarding the revision of its Indigenous Peoples' Policy, welcome the willingness of the Bank to engage in dialogue with indigenous peoples on ways to address our priorities and our concerns relating to the policy revision.

We wish to contribute to this dialogue by presenting several minimum principles that we consider must be applied in the final revised policy in order to ensure that the Bank adopts an effective safeguard policy that will respect, promote and protect the rights of indigenous peoples in World Bank-assisted development operations. The following points do not comprise the full set of standards upon which we insist, but express some of our central concerns and priorities.

We maintain that, to be effective, any revised safeguard policy must contain clear mandatory provisions that:

- Rights of indigenous peoples recognised at the international level:
  - Are consistent with existing international human rights standards, including, for example, the UN Charter, the Universal Declaration on Human Rights, the International Covenant on Civil and Political Rights, the International Covenant on Economic, Social and Cultural Rights, CERD, Convention on the Rights of the Child, the ILO Convention 169, the Draft UN Declaration on the Rights of Indigenous Peoples, the Draft American Declaration on the Rights of Indigenous Peoples, as well as principles in other relevant international standards on indigenous rights such as those contained in the Convention on Biological Diversity;
  - Prohibit World Bank funding of projects or programmes that risk contravening the borrowers'

international obligations on human rights and the environment;

- ❖ Uphold the Bank's obligations under international law to recognise, protect and reinforce the human rights of indigenous peoples;

- Policy coverage:
  - ❖ Apply the principle of self-identification as a fundamental element in determining the scope and coverage of the policy;
  - ❖ Extend the coverage of the policy to address structural adjustment and programmatic lending.

- Participation and accountability:
  - ❖ Require prior and participatory baseline studies in all instances in which a Bank project or program will affect indigenous peoples, our territories or our communities;
  - ❖ Include requirements for involving local, national and regional indigenous organisations in active tracking and monitoring of World Bank operations through the whole project cycle;
  - ❖ Require enforceable legal covenants in loan agreements between the World Bank, borrower governments and affected indigenous peoples;
  - ❖ Require the effective collective participation by indigenous peoples affected by Bank loan operations throughout the project cycle (design, preparation and implementation);
  - ❖ Recognise the right of indigenous peoples to free, prior and informed consent, including our right to say "no", to any developments proposals that may affect our territories and lands;
  - ❖ Ensure the equitable and effective participation of indigenous representatives in the governance of projects and programmes to which they have given their prior consent;
  - ❖ Establish accessible and responsive accountability mechanisms on the ground.

- Land and natural resources:
  - Recognise and protect indigenous peoples' ownership and property rights over their territories, lands and resources in accordance with the customary law, values, usage, and customs of affected communities;
  - Require Bank staff and Borrowers to take action to safeguard and guarantee the rights of indigenous peoples to our territories, lands and resources;
  - Prohibit involuntary resettlement of indigenous peoples and stipulate that resettlement may only take place with the full, prior, free and informed consent of affected indigenous communities.

We value this Round table discussion as an important step in our continuing efforts to ensure that the international development system upholds and protects indigenous peoples' rights. However, we reiterate that this meeting is only the beginning of a dialogue between indigenous peoples and the World Bank.

We, therefore, request that the adoption of the revised policy be postponed until and unless there is a clear understanding and consensus on this issue that reflects the views and priorities of indigenous peoples from all parts of the world.

Note

1. It is interesting to note that even before the countries and governments could evolve any policy on the Indigenous Peoples, international financial institutions like the World Bank have come out with policies on Indigenous Peoples. Knowing this well, the Indigenous Peoples have responded to these policies.

9

The International Cancun Declaration of Indigenous Peoples

5th WTO Ministerial Conference - Cancun, Quintana Roo, Mexico, 12 September 2003

We, the international representatives of Indigenous Peoples gathered here during the 5th WTO Ministerial Conference in Cancun[1], Mexico from 10-14 September 2003 wish to extend our thanks to the Indigenous Peoples of Mexico, particularly the Mayan Indigenous Peoples of Quintana Roo, for welcoming us.

We share the concerns of our Indigenous brothers and sisters, as expressed in the Congress National Indigenous Declaration of Cancun. We join our voices to this CNI Declaration and its conclusions and recommendations.

We wish to especially recognise and honour the sacrifice of our Korean brother, Mr. Lee-Kyung-Hae, made here in Cancun. His act of self-immolation was a dignified cultural expression profoundly reflecting the daily reality of the effects of Globalisation and liberalised trade on peasants and Indigenous Peoples throughout the world.

We have come to Cancun to address critical issues and negative impacts of WTO Trade Negotiations on our families, communities and nations.

With the creation of WTO and with the continuing imposition of the structural adjustment policies of the World

Bank and IMF, our situation, as Indigenous Peoples, has turned from bad to worse. Corporations are given more rights and privileges at the expense of our rights. Our right to self-determination, which is to freely determine our political status and pursue our own economic, social and cultural development, and our rights to our territories and resources, to our indigenous knowledge, cultures and identities are grossly violated. Some of the prime examples of the adverse impacts of the WTO Agreements on us are the following:

Loss of livelihoods of hundreds of thousands of indigenous peasants in Mexico who are producing corn because of the dumping of artificially cheap, highly subsidised corn from the USA and tens of thousands of indigenous vegetable producers in the Cordillera region of the Philippines because of dumping of vegetables. The contamination of traditional indigenous corn in Mexico by genetically modified corn is a very serious problem for Indigenous Peoples. All these are due to the liberalisation of trade in agriculture and the deregulation of laws, which protect domestic producers and crops required by WTO's AOA. The structural adjustment policies of the World Bank and IMF are the foundations for liberalisation, privatisation and deregulation. High export subsidies and domestic support provided to rich agribusiness corporations and rich farmers in the United States the European Union have also made this possible.

The increasing impoverishment of indigenous and hill tribe farmers engaged in coffee production in Guatemala, Mexico, Colombia, Vietnam, etc. because of the drop in commodity prices of coffee.

The increasing conflicts between transnational mining, gas and oil corporations and Indigenous Peoples in the Philippines, Indonesia, Papua New Guinea, India, Ecuador, Guyana, Venezuela, Colombia, Nigeria, Chad-Cameroon, USA, Russia, Venezuela, among others, and the militarisation and environmental devastation in these communities due to the operations of these extractive industries. The facilitation of the entry of such corporations are made possible because of liberalisation of investment laws pushed by TRIMS Agreement and WB-IMF conditionality, regional trade agreements like NAFTA and bilateral investment agreements.

The militarisation of Indigenous Peoples' lands and territories, and the many cases of assassination and arbitrary arrests and detention of indigenous activists and leaders and people who are supporting them, as well as the criminalisation of Indigenous Peoples' resistance, all significantly increased.

The upsurge in infrastructure development, particularly of mega hydroelectric dams, oil and gas pipelines, roads in Indigenous Peoples territories to provide support to operations of extractive industries, logging corporations, and export processing zones. The infrastructure development, for instance, under Plan Panama has destroyed ceremonial and sacred sites of Indigenous Peoples in the six States of Southern Mexico and in Guatemala.

The patenting of medicinal plants and seeds nurtured and used by Indigenous Peoples, like the *quinoa, ayahuasca*, Mexican yellow bean, *maca, sangre de drago, hoodia*, yew plant, etc. Such biopiracy and patenting of life forms is facilitated by the TRIPS Agreement.

Soaring prices of pharmaceutical products and inaccessibility of cheaper drugs for diseases like tuberculosis, malaria, AIDS which are diseases in Indigenous Peoples communities and decreasing public health services in these communities.

Privatisation of basic public services such as water and energy in several countries which has spurred massive general strikes and protests such as those led by Indigenous Peoples in Bolivia. GATS, whose coverage is being expanded to include environmental services (sanitation, nature and landscape protection), financial services, tourism, among others, allowed for this.

The undermining of international instruments, constitutional provisions, and national laws and policies, which protect our rights.

All these developments are alarming. This global situation has undermined self-sufficient economies of Indigenous Peoples leading to food insecurity, worsening poverty and loss of land, culture and identity. We, the Indigenous Peoples' representatives, present in Cancun during the event of the

Fifth Ministerial Meeting of WTO, are asking the governments to do the following:

Recognise and protect our territorial and resource rights and our right to self-determination. The human-rights framework should underpin trade, investment, development and anti-poverty policies and programmes. Investment liberalisation rules like the TRIMS Agreement, conditionality by the WB and IMF, which push countries to liberalise their investment laws, regional trade agreements, and bilateral investment agreements, which give more protection and rights to corporations than to Indigenous Peoples, should be changed. Many of these facilitate the displacement of Indigenous Peoples and the appropriation of our lands, waters, resources and knowledge. Indigenous peoples who have been displaced from their lands because of militarisation, infrastructure projects, extractive industries, export processing zones and other development schemes should be repatriated back to their lands or should be justly compensated. International human rights and environmental standards should be upheld by governments, and should guide the way trade agreements are formulated and implemented. The free and prior informed consent of Indigenous Peoples should be obtained before any project is brought into their communities. Article 8j and 10c of the Convention of Biological Diversity that protect traditional knowledge and indigenous systems and practices of land use and land tenure should be the framework for WTO Agreements. Governments should support the immediate adoption of the UN Draft Declaration on the Rights of Indigenous Peoples that will help ensure the recognition and protection of our rights.

Stop patenting of life forms and other intellectual property rights over biological resources and indigenous knowledge. Ensure that we, the Indigenous Peoples, retain our rights to have control over our seeds, medicinal plants and indigenous knowledge.

We call for an explicit statement for the banning of patents on life forms in TRIPS Agreement. We also demand that the patent rights, patent applications and claims of corporations, individuals or governments over indigenous medicinal plants, seeds, and knowledge and even over Indigenous Peoples' human genetic materials should be withdrawn. Biopiracy should be stopped and the free and prior informed consent of Indigenous Peoples should be obtained before access to their resources is granted. WTO TRIPs Agreement should not deal with the issue of protection of indigenous knowledge because its basic assumptions contradict the concepts, values and ethics underpinning indigenous knowledge systems. This can be best protected under the United Nations and we therefore, urge the UN Permanent Forum on Indigenous Issues to convene a technical meeting to explore how the UN can address the issue of protection of indigenous knowledge.

Ensure Indigenous Peoples' basic right to health. The right of countries to take measures to protect public health and promote access to medicines should take precedence over their obligations to protect intellectual property right of corporations. The patent protection asked by pharmaceutical and biotechnology corporations should be limited in order to protect public health and safety and ensure production and easy access to cheap essential medicines. Health is a basic human right and Indigenous Peoples should enjoy this right. Governments should be allowed to use the flexibilities allowed in the TRIPS Agreement, which are reflected in the Doha TRIPS and Public Health Declaration. An amendment to TRIPS should be done to simplify and clarify the procedures for compulsory licensing and parallel importation and to remove the unnecessary obstacles to the import and export of medicines needed to provide affordable medicines to the poor.

No new issues should be negotiated in this 5th Ministerial Conference. We support the position of some developing countries to stop the launching of a new round or to expand the WTO by negotiating on new issues such as investments, competition, and transparency in government procurement and trade facilitation. The WTO should not pursue any negotiation on investment and should change its existing investment rules, which provide excessive rights to corporations and allow for their unregulated behavior. Those rules, which prevent governments from pursuing rights-based development and environmentally sustainable policies, should be abandoned.

Prevent the expansion of GATS Agreement and amend the existing agreement to stop privatisation and liberalisation of health, education, water, energy, and environmental services. The liberalisation and privatisation of services in environmental services (e.g. parks and landscape services), the commercialisation of indigenous cultures and the increasing monopoly control of the tourism industry in the hands of international and national travel and tour agencies should be stopped. We must be allowed to be the managers of protected areas, parks, forests and waters found in our territories. We should be able to continue practicing our own indigenous natural management practices in forests, water, and biodiversity and ecosystem management.

Stop the negotiations on agriculture, which will push for further import of agricultural products. Drastically end the export and domestic subsidies of the US and the EU for their agribusiness corporations and rich farmers. States must take decisive measures to promote and protect food sovereignty and food security, and stop the dumping and smuggling of artificially cheap and highly subsidised agricultural products from the US, EU, Canada, Australia and New Zealand. Ensure the right of indigenous farmers to sustain their indigenous agricultural systems and to plant and reproduce their traditional seeds. States must not include indigenous agriculture systems in the scope of international trade rules. The rights of Indigenous Peoples to their traditional livelihoods and to food should be recognised and protected; thus, trade and investment rules, which undermine these rights, should be repealed or appropriately amended.

End the militarisation of Indigenous Peoples' communities and stop the criminalisation of protest and resistance actions of Indigenous Peoples against destructive industries, projects and programs. There should be meaningful and effective investigation of the many cases of assassinations, arbitrary arrests and detentions, rapes committed against Indigenous Peoples and their supporters. Justice should be accorded to the victims and their families, and the perpetrators punished for their crimes.

Support and strengthen the sustainable trading systems, which have existed for centuries between the Indigenous Peoples of the Americas. Trade routes between the various Indigenous Peoples within the Americas (USA, Canada, Mexico) have been existing for centuries and trading between them is still practiced, Militarisation of borders and other destructive practices have greatly limited their scale and utility for Indigenous Peoples. Trade between Indigenous Peoples should be sustained and promoted.

The ministers at this Fifth Ministerial meeting of WTO have the responsibility to represent not only commercial interests but also all of the people of their States, including Indigenous Peoples. Existing human rights, environmental, social and cultural conventions and covenants developed within the United Nations system continue to be the States' legal if not moral obligation. All international law, including human rights law, binds them.

Indigenous peoples are the subjects of many of these covenants and conventions and their jurisprudence. Our rights cannot be ignored, nor can their observance be diminished or compromised by trade agreements and regimes. We as Indigenous Peoples have the right to participate as peoples and actors in our own development, consistent with our own vision and tradition. Our free and informed consent, free of fraud or manipulation, must be secured through our own traditional means of decision-making. State sponsored development cannot just be imposed upon us. Our rights as peoples to our lands and territories and natural resources must be recognised, respected and observed. Our survival as peoples depends upon it.

Signatories:

Name of Organisation Country

1. Asian Indigenous Women's Network
2. Cordillera Peoples Alliance Philippines
3. Indigenous Environmental Network
4. Indigenous Initiative for Peace
5. Indigenous Women's Network
6. International Indian Treaty Council
7. Na Koa Ikaika Kalahui Hawaii
8. Tebtebba Foundation

Note

1. The Indigenous Peoples did not let go any opportunity to present their case for self-determination. For example, when the 5th WTO Ministerial Conference took place in Cancun in Mexico, the representatives of the Indigenous Peoples gathered to present their view that all these trade agreements under mine self-sufficiencies of the Indigenous Peoples and their communities.

10

Toward a Consensus of the Peoples

Issued at the Latin American gathering of Indigenous and Tribal Leaders and their Allies

Mexico City, 6-9 December 2003

We, coming from 15 countries of three continents, came together over several days in Mexico City, to reflect together about our relations and perspectives.

We cannot talk in the name of the communities and peoples to which we belong, and even less in the name of all of the peoples of the continent. We believe nevertheless, that the fabric of ideas and attitudes that we have been weaving in the course of our conversations is inspired by them and perhaps can inspire others.

We are suffering, like many others, the consequences of neoliberal policies. Capital has more appetite than ever, but not enough stomach to digest the many it wants to control. Millions people are becoming unnecessary, disposable. The constituted powers all over the world, allied to the transnational corporations, blindly apply the senseless policies of the so-called Washington consensus, at an unsupportable human and environmental cost.

More than these evils, known to all of us, we talked about who we are, and of what we form in a rich mosaic of many 'we's' that define us. We talked about the attitudes that make us be what we are, of the difficulties that we confront, of our dreams and of the meaning of our struggles.

The conclusions that we reached are only a moment of reflection on a path that we started some time ago, and on which we continue walking. One of these conclusions is that it seems that there is in the process of formation, at the grassroots, a consensus among the Indigenous Peoples.

CONSENSUS OF THE PEOPLES

This consensus, if it effectively would be reached, could articulate and connect their activities, with the full respect to the diversity and autonomy of each community and people, who can live this consensus in different ways. We hope that others, particularly in the communities, can enrich what we have woven so far, which has, among other things, the following elements.

1. Radical Pluralism. We want to create a world in which many worlds can be embraced. That the dissolution of cultures and peoples in order to integrate them into one design on the terms of the old western project of domination is stopped. We want a world in which the cultural differences are appreciated and respected and coexist in harmony, starting from a radical pluralist attitude.
2. Personal Dignity. We celebrate the dignity of each man and woman, who nurture the dignity of their peoples and cultures. With a basis in it, the richness of their diversity will flourish. Expanding personal and cultural dignity will be a challenge to all the existing political and economic systems, and will demonstrate that they have an oppressive, unjust and irrational character.
3. Autonomy. Our de facto autonomy of our communities and peoples is an expression our dignity. We will continue to struggle until we reach their legal recognition. From the Laws of the Indies, in what today is Latin America, the legal machinery has always been at the service of the powerful and the bad government. The courts are a travesty of justice. Without abandoning our internal normative systems, we will continue to vindicate the

legal and political process, together they constitute the structure of freedom. Our autonomy will be recognised by the law.

4. New Political Regime. The constitutional recognition of the existence, autonomy and self determination of the peoples who form the most profound layer of our societies, will create a new political regime that leaves behind the structure of domination inherent in the nation state. Such regime should be supported by the sovereignty of the people and preserve it, even in the current global disorder.
5. Subordinate the economy. We want to reestablish politics and ethics as the center of social life, exorcising the economic obsession of the dominant system, that only concentrates privileges in the few. Instead of submitting needs and desires to the competitive fury of the great economic powers, to feed their voracity, we will put the operation of the economy at the service of the people, the community and the peoples.
6. Radical Democracy. Before the current disenchantment, with so called formal democracy, in which political parties and government show themselves to be unable to lead the collective efforts in a just social order, we want to affirm ourselves in the radical democracy of our communitarian traditions, that weave a consensus at the grassroots. Democracy can only be where the people are, in communities, neighborhoods, and peoples. From them we are reconstructing society, with the participation of everyone, in order to generate new social and political consensus.
7. Conviviality. We generate a convivial order of life in our communities and neighbourhoods. We will not let consumer society, in which he who is not a prisoner of the addiction to products and services he has learned to consume falls victim to envy for those he cannot afford, dissolve it.
8. Communality. Confronting the possessive individualism that continues to affect our daily lives, we raise communality, as a condition of harmony in coexistence,

with plain respect for liberty and the rights of peoples.

9. Create a New World. To change the world, and all of its oppressive institutions is very difficult, if not impossible. It seems however viable to create a new world that is economically feasible, socially just, and ecologically sound. Those of us who have not let ourselves be tied down by forces and structures that seem unstoppable and pretend to dominate everything are already doing it.
10. Autonomy in exchange. We resist the false choice between 'free trade' and 'protectionism'. One hands over power to the corporations, the other to the bureaucrats who are at the service of the first. 'Protectionism' does not protect the people. 'Free Trade' does not respect our freedom. Exchanges have to be controlled autonomously by the people, so that the people themselves determine what they prefer.
11. Socialisation. We resist equally 'privatisation' and 'statisation' ('nationalisation'). We are looking for socialisation of goods and services, constructed on the basis of autonomy. It is insane and unjust to turn over social resources and public services to private voracity. Bureaucratic monopolies are not an efficient or appropriate alternative. We trust, however, in a dencetralised and autonomous administration of goods and general services, with the participation of the citizens.
12. Service and Reciprocity. We want the strengthening and articulation of the coalitions of the discontent with the dominant system. From them, we widen our interactions to construct alternatives, to learn from one another and to offer mutual solidarity.

Signatories:

Argentina: Jorge Nahuel Werken; Bolivia: Alvaro García Linera, Evo Morales, Félix Patzi, Felipe Quispe, Leonilda Zurita; Canada: Kalpana Das, Agusti Nicolau; Colombia: Alfredo Acosta, Abadio Green Stocel, Eder Sánchez; Chile: José María Bulnes, José Naín; Costa Rica: Levi Sucre; Ecuador: Felipe Burbano, Leonidas Iza, Miguel Lluco, Roberto Restrepo; Guatemala: Domingo Hernández Ixcuy, Guadalupe García

Hernández, Fabiana Gómez, Pedro Marchetti; India: Smitu Kothari; México: Rodolfo Stavenhagen, Joel Aquino, Juan Chávez, Aldo González, Pedro Gutiérrez Jiménez, Francisco López Bárcenas, Adelfo Regino, Sofía Robles, Marcos Sandoval, Alicia Barabas, Miguel Bartolomé, Ana Esther Ceceña José del Val, Fabiola Escárzaga, Gustavo Esteva, Néstor García Canclini, Magdalena Gómez, John Holloway, Miguel León Portilla, Alfredo López Austin, Benjamín Maldonado, Carlos Montemayor, Salomón Nahmad, Mercedes Olivera, Antonio Paoli, Carlos Plascencia, José Ricardo Robles, Héctor Rosales, Raymundo Sánchez Barraza, Martha Sánchez, Luis Villoro, Pablo Yanes; New Zealand: Peter Horsley; Perú: Juan José García Miranda, Marcela Machaca, Grimaldo Rengifo; United States of America: Gustavo Terán, William Underbaggage.

11

The Asian Development Bank's Indigenous Peoples' Policy and its Impact on Indigenous Peoples of Asia

Raja Devasish Roy[1]

The Scope of the Policy

The policy of ADB indigenous peoples is triggered when negative impacts of an ADB-supported project are anticipated.[2] In such a situation, 'adequate measures must be taken to mitigate the negative impact, or make certain that a compensation plan ensuring that project-affected people are as well off with the project as without it'.[3] The policy applies to both public and private sector operations.[4] It defines or identifies indigenous peoples in a broad manner and includes one or more of the following:

- Descent from pre-state population groups.
- Maintenance of cultural and other identities, institutions, etc. that are distinct from mainstream society.
- Self-identification, identification by others and desire to maintain its cultural identity.
- Distinct linguistic identity.
- Orientation towards traditional economic systems.
- Attachment to traditional habitats and territories.[5]

In addition, a working definition is employed as an

operational tool, which reads: "*Indigenous peoples should be regarded as those with a social or cultural identity distinct from the dominant or mainstream society, which makes them vulnerable to being disadvantaged in the process of development.*"[6]

The ambit or scope of the application of ADB's policy on indigenous peoples is clarified in the document itself, which states: "*The policy, together with practices addressing indigenous peoples, applies in parallel with and does not replace or supersede other ADB policies and practices. Each of the elements of the policy and practice addressing indigenous peoples are considered within the context of national development policies and approaches, and the fundamental relationship between ADB and governments remains the basis for country-specific operations (emphasis added).*"[7]

To rephrase the above, the policy itself advises us that in order to understand the full implications of ADB-funded projects upon indigenous peoples, we must look, in addition to the specific policy itself, into the following: (a) other relevant ADB policies; (b) relevant ADB practices; (c) development policies and approaches of the borrower government; and (d) the nature of the relationship between the ADB and the concerned borrower government.

Therefore, it appears that although the ADB's indigenous peoples' policy applies equally to all its member countries, the nature of its actual impact on the ground would *vary from country to country*. It would depend upon such factors as the bank's numerous policies and practices in addition to its *Indigenous Peoples'* policy, the relevant policies and practices of the borrower governments and the dynamics of the ADB-borrower relationship. Case studies of field-level experiences related to ADB-funded projects in areas inhabited by indigenous peoples would provide added insights into the matter under study.

Basic Elements of the Policy

One of the salient elements of ADB's Indigenous Peoples' Policy is to 'avoid negatively impacting indigenous peoples' through ADB operations. Where that is not possible, the policy is to provide 'adequate and appropriate compensation'.[8] When substantial negative impacts on indigenous peoples are anticipated, the first step is to conduct an *Initial Social Assessment* (ISA), which is mandatory for all ADB projects.[9] The policy recommends that ISA be initiated in the early stages of a project.[10] ISA addresses the key social dimensions of the project, as well as the needs, demands and capacities of the people concerned.[11] It also identifies the project beneficiaries and the people that are likely to be adversely affected by the concerned project.[12]

If ISA determines that indigenous peoples are likely to be adversely impacted, or that indigenous peoples suffer from disadvantage or are otherwise vulnerable in the project intervention process, *an Indigenous Peoples' Development Plan* must be prepared by the borrower government or other project sponsor, to address the relevant needs or disadvantage, as the case may be.[13] Where appropriate, the Indigenous Peoples Development Plan is expected to redesign a project in order to decrease or mitigate negative impacts, or to provide adequate compensation, in addition to mitigating harm or damage.[14] The policy recognises that consultation with indigenous peoples' groups is 'key to developing an effective, accurate, and responsive indigenous peoples development plan'. Consequently, it appears to consider consultation with affected peoples as mandatory.[15] The elaborate provisions on the Indigenous Peoples Development Plan include suggestions to consider the wishes of the affected indigenous peoples and their social and cultural patterns, capacity building of the concerned communities, organisations and institutions, and the use of specialists to help formulate such plans.[16]

Positive and Negative Features of the Policy and its Application

As is the case with various other instruments dealing with the issues of indigenous peoples', the ADB policy on indigenous peoples contains positive features or strengths, as well as weaknesses and gaps that could be regarded as the policy's 'negative' features. *Weaknesses and Negative Features* One of the most serious gaps or weaknesses in the policy is the general treatment of the policy at par with other policies of the bank, since the policy 'applies in parallel with and does not replace or supercede other ADB policies and practices'.[17] Therefore, theoretically, if there is a contradiction between the bank's *Indigenous Peoples' Policy* and another ADB policy or practice, the former (the *Indigenous Peoples' Policy*) will not necessarily prevail, and this can work to the detriment of indigenous peoples.

This was the case, for example, with the ADB's forestry sector support to the Government of Bangladesh, in which the provisions of the bank's Forestry policy prevailed over its *Indigenous Peoples' Policy*.[18] In addition, the bank's other relevant policies and practices must be considered "within the context of national development policies and approaches", since 'the fundamental relationship between ADB and governments remains the basis for country-specific operations'.[19]

In other words, despite provisions in the ADB's *Indigenous Peoples' Policy* respecting indigenous peoples' rights, needs and concerns, if national development policies and approaches of the borrower country run counter to these, the latter could well defeat, or water down, the impact of the positive aspects of the policy. In fact, this is quite a common occurrence across Asia.

For instance, indigenous peoples on the ground rejected a number of forestry sector legal reforms in Bangladesh because these denied the people's land and resource rights. The reforms were facilitated by ADB Technical Assistance (TA) grants, which are provided in relation to past, ongoing and future loans. Many of the provisions of the national forestry policy of Bangladesh were in conflict with the positive aspects of the bank's *Indigenous Peoples' Policy*.[20] Similarly, another ADB-funded social forestry project in Bangladesh, which also affected indigenous peoples, was deemed to have paid little heed to the rights of women.[21]

These examples from Bangladesh illustrate how the differing nature and level of protection provided by the ADB's *Indigenous Peoples' Policy,* and other policies and practices of the bank can lead to minimal protection of indigenous peoples' rights. Such protection could even verge towards a *lowest common denominator* situation, rather than strongly and unequivocally upholding the rights of indigenous peoples. In contrast, the *Indigenous Peoples' Policies* of some non-lending donor institutions, such as the Government of Denmark and the European Commission, provide a far higher status to the rights of indigenous peoples.[22] Of course, one should bear in mind that the Danish government and the European Commission are non-profit institutions. The ADB, although an inter-governmental agency, is managed as a profit-making corporation. Its major decision making processes are dominated by the strong corporate shareholdings of the different national governments in Asia and other continents.

Strengths and Positive Features

Despite the weaknesses and gaps of the ADB *Indigenous Peoples' Policy,* as mentioned above, a number of other provisions are respectful of the rights of indigenous peoples. These positive provisions have the potential to secure the rights and interests of indigenous peoples, at least in the limited circumstance where the bank and the loanee government are in agreement. The policy states the following:

" .. initiatives should be compatible in substance and structure with the affected peoples' culture and social and economic institutions, and commensurate with the needs, aspirations, and demands of affected peoples. Initiatives should be conceived, planned and implemented, to the maximum extent possible, with the informed consent of affected communities, and include respect for indigenous peoples' dignity, human rights and cultural uniqueness".[23]

Another positive feature of the policy is the acknowledgment of the disadvantaged situation of indigenous peoples. It also refers to international instruments on indigenous peoples' rights and recommends involving and strengthening indigenous peoples' institutions in the Indigenous Peoples Development Plan.[24]

Difficulties, however, lie in the process of implementation. The ADB does not provide parallel mechanisms to ensure that the previously mentioned positive provisions are regarded as mandatory. A similar situation prevails in the case of the *World Bank Indigenous Peoples'* Policy, which bears striking similarities with the ADB's. Recent reforms to the World Bank's *Indigenous Peoples'* Policy – the replacement of OD 4.20 by OP

4.10/BP 4.10 – include many desirable provisions that respect indigenous peoples' rights. However, these appear to be merely recommendatory, rather than mandatory.[25]

Well-researched and objective findings on the positive impacts of ADB-funded development program on indigenous peoples are hard to find. The scarce literature that show ADB interventions in indigenous peoples' areas in a positive light appear to have been initiated or facilitated by the bank itself. In Bangladesh, for example, ADB-funded projects are generally regarded as harmful rather than beneficial to indigenous peoples.[26] Nevertheless, the possibility of positive and creative use of the policy to safeguard indigenous peoples' rights and interests should not be ruled out.

Case Study: A Potentially Positive ADB Project Intervention for Indigenous People; The Chittagong Hill Tracts Rural Development Project in Bangladesh A *potentially* positive example of ADB intervention, with support from the indigenous people of the area concerned, is the *Chittagong Hill Tracts Rural Development Project* in Bangladesh.[27]

The project was initiated with the consent of the Chittagong Hill Tracts Regional Council, the premier indigenous-majority semi-autonomous institution of the Chittagong Hill Tracts region. The project includes the indigenous chairperson of this council as the *ex-officio* chairperson of the project's *Regional Coordination Committee*, with three indigenous district council chairpersons and the three traditional paramount chiefs as members.[28] The project's primary focus is to reduce 'absolute poverty' in the Chittagong Hill Tracts region and to provide a confidence-building environment to underpin the Chittagong Hill Tracts Peace Accord of 1997. The project also includes a *Community Development* component with programs on *Legal Literacy*, *Training* and *Gender.*[29] The loan agreement between the bank and the Government of Bangladesh refers to the monitoring and implementation of an *Indigenous Peoples' Development Plan* by the project-monitoring unit.[30]

The involvement of representative institutions of indigenous peoples in decision-making and project implementation is no doubt a desirable development, if that has happened with the prior, informed consent of the peoples concerned. However, the potentially positive impact of the project is at risk of being diluted, or even undone, by certain features of the project that have been included without the knowledge and consent of the peoples concerned. In particular, the inclusion into the project of micro-credit disbursement by local NGOs was apparently done at the behest of the bank's president rather than by the wishes of the indigenous peoples of the region.[31] At a recent meeting of the *Regional Coordination Committee*, serious concerns were raised by the chairperson and other indigenous members regarding the proposed loan disbursement, which is in violation of regional laws, practices and interests of local indigenous people.[32]

Monitoring, Evaluation and Policy Review: Weaknesses and Opportunities

An important factor in ensuring the implementation of the positive features of the ADB *Indigenous Peoples' Policy* is effective monitoring. This, in turn, is dependent on the bank's *internal* mechanisms and processes of monitoring and evaluation, as well as on the external processes of monitoring and evaluation by indigenous peoples, governments, and NGOs. With regard to internal monitoring, the bank's most important agencies are the *Office of Environment and Social Development (OESD)*, the *Programmes Department* (in relation to country programming), the resident missions in the countries, and the *Operations Evaluation Office*, the last-named being involved predominantly in 'post-evaluation' functions.[33]

However, it appears that these agencies do not have much influence on the bank's operations in indigenous people-inhabited areas, except in limited circumstances such as the project in the Chittagong Hill Tracts region in Bangladesh. In the case of the *Office of Environment and Social Development*, individual employees may have the required attitude and respect for indigenous peoples' rights, aspirations and perspectives. However, their views seem to run counter to those of other weightier departments and agencies within the bank. The situation is best illustrated by a comment made informally by a World Bank employee. He lamented, *"What can we, a dozen or so sociologists and anthropologists, do in the wake of contrary views of our more influential economist colleagues, whose numbers run into the hundreds, and whose primary concerns have little to do with the welfare of indigenous peoples or other such groups..."*[34]

In any future revision of ADB's *Indigenous Peoples' Policy*, the findings of the ADB *Operations Evaluation Office*, if obtained in an accurate and objective manner, would be of great assistance. In the case of World Bank, the bank ignored or missed a similar opportunity to disseminate and utilise the findings of its corresponding agency, the Operations Evaluation Department, during appropriate stages of its *Indigenous Peoples' Policy* revision process.[35]

Therefore, a crucial factor in determining proper implementation, monitoring and evaluation, and consequent revision, is the question of how participatory the bank's approach is in involving indigenous peoples in the relevant processes. Opportunities can always be created to open the necessary space for indigenous perspectives, if the bank's high-level decision-makers can muster the will to do so. The ADB has formally consulted indigenous peoples and other "stakeholders" in the process of policy formulation,[36] and policy-review in certain cases.[37] However, these processes are generally inadequate in terms of time and opportunity given to indigenous peoples and other *stakeholders* to provide their inputs.[38] Only a few of these processes were sufficiently inclusive or transparent.[39]

Unless such trends are corrected, indigenous peoples will remain substantively deprived of their rights in ADB-financed projects and interventions in their areas. The example of the World Bank's consultation process for its recently reformed *Indigenous Peoples'* Policy was one of inadequate consultation and sensitivity.[40] The experience suggests that indigenous peoples need to strengthen their lobbying efforts, if they are to influence reforms in policy and practice of multilateral development banks in the right direction. It would do well to remember that, ultimately, institutions such as ADB and WB are primarily oriented towards profit. Their perspective of economic growth through a 'poverty reduction' is insufficiently receptive of indigenous perspectives on rights and development.

Despite such limitations, indigenous peoples can strengthen their networking and organisational skills, and help steer policy reforms in their hoped-for direction through advocacy, lobbying and policy dialogue. With this as a backdrop, a number of observations are made below, which can facilitate indigenous people's efforts to change the relevant policies and practices of the ADB. This change is necessary in order to bring the policies and practice of the ADB in conformity with the existing and emerging international standards on the rights of indigenous peoples.

Conclusion: Ways Forward

- *Reform the Existing Policy*

There is much room to improve upon the contents of the policy itself. The current policy accounts for the rights of indigenous peoples, without an unequivocal commitment to honor and respect these rights. More importantly, the policy does not provide adequate mechanisms to respect and adhere to such rights. The basic rights of indigenous peoples, including their right to self-determination, their rights over their lands and territories, and their right to prior and informed consent[41] concerning development interventions in their areas are now part of customary international law. These need to be unequivocally acknowledged as part of mandatory guidelines in any policy revision.

- *Process of Review and Reform*

Although ADB did consult a limited number of indigenous peoples' representatives prior to the adoption of its current *Indigenous Peoples' Policy*, such consultations were regarded by indigenous peoples as inadequate.[42] The process of reforming the bank's Forestry policy, for example, was seriously flawed by being insufficiently open, transparent or inclusive.[43] Similarly to be avoided is the manner in which the World Bank held formal consultations with indigenous peoples' representatives, including legal experts, between 2002-2005.[44] The modalities for a future review process of ADBs *Indigenous Peoples' Policy* need to be agreed upon, together with indigenous peoples. Such consultations need to be preceded by an indepth evaluation of the diverse impacts of ADB-funded projects on indigenous peoples.

• *Monitoring and Evaluation of Project Impact upon Indigenous Peoples*

The experience of the European Commission (EC) in having some of its projects evaluated by indigenous experts, and the findings shared among indigenous peoples and EC project staff and policy-level officials, can provide ideas for similar evaluation exercises of ADB-funded projects. Indigenous peoples have demanded that the World Bank involve local, national and regional indigenous organisations in actively tracking and monitoring its operations throughout the whole project cycle.[45] Such needs are equally relevant in the case of the ADB.

• *Influencing Policy Reforms by ADB-Member Country Governments*

Since the ADB's *Indigenous Peoples' Policy* is affected by the relevant policies of the borrower governments, the positive impact of the bank's policy would be watered down or countered in the absence of adequate acknowledgement of indigenous peoples' rights in national laws and policies. Some have advocated that ADB engage the concerned national governments to initiate policy reforms in their countries and to effectively implement the bank's *Policy on Indigenous Peoples.*[46] It is important in this respect to encourage ADB member governments to not only consult indigenous peoples, but to institutionalise appropriate methods of consultation.[47]

• *Information and Data*

Dissemination of data and information (in appropriate form) is crucial to ensuring that the necessary implementation and reform process is in accordance with the rights of indigenous peoples. This can also promote transparency and accountability.[48]

• *Including Indigenous Peoples in Bank-Member Country Negotiations*

The ADB policy clearly declares that "the fundamental relationship between the ADB and governments remain the basis for country-specific operations".[49] Indigenous peoples are, however, often unaware of the contractual relationship between the bank and borrower governments. This problem needs to be corrected through indigenous participation, both in the deliberations of the bank and in policy dialogues with the concerned government.[50]

Notes

1. The writer is the Chief of the Chakma Administrative Circle in the Chittagong Hill Tracts (CHT), Bangladesh, an adviser to the Ministry of CHT Affairs, and is associated with various indigenous peoples' and development organisations.
2. Asian Development Bank, *Policy on Indigenous Peoples*, pp., 2, 9.
3. *Ibid.*
4. *Ibid.*, p. 17.
5. *Ibid*, p. 6.
6. *Ibid.* Case-specific identification may also be addressed at the stage of *Initial Social Assessment*. See also, pp. 6, 7 and Appendix.
7. *Ibid*, p. 25. The same paragraph further provides the following (at p. 25): 'The strategies and approaches employed by ADB in relation to indigenous peoples build on the existing strategic framework and operational experience. The policy addressing indigenous peoples complements and supports, and is complemented and supported by other ADB policies. Compliance with the policy on indigenous peoples does not obviate the requirement of compliance with other ADB policies'.
8. *Ibid.*
9. *Ibid.*, p. 18. See further, (i) *Guidelines for Incorporation of Social Dimensions in Bank Operations,* Asian Development Bank, Manila, October, 1993; (ii) *Handbook for Incorporation of Social Dimensions in Projects*, Asian Development Bank, Manila, May, 1994.
10. *Ibid*, p. 18.
11. *Ibid.*
12. *Ibid.*, p. 18, 19.
13. *Ibid.*, pp. 19, 20.
14. *Ibid.*, p. 19.
15. *Ibid.*, p. 28 (Appendix).
16. *Ibid.*
17. *Ibid.*, p. 25.
18. Philip Gain, *Background and Context to the Forest (Amendment) Act, 2000 and the (draft) Social Forestry Rules, 2000,* Society for

Environment and Human Development (SEHD), Dhaka, Bangladesh, May, 2001, and Raja Devasish Roy & Philip Gain, "Indigenous Peoples and Forests in Bangladesh" in Minority Rights Group (ed.), *Forests and Indigenous Peoples of Asia,* Report 98/4, London, 1999, pp. 21-22.

19. *Ibid.*

20. Raja Devasish Roy and Sadeka Halim, "A Critique to the Forest (Amendment) Act of 2000 and (Draft) Social Forestry Rules of 2000", published by Society for Environment and Human Development (SEHD), Dhaka, Bangladesh, May, 2001. Philip Gain, *Background and Context to the Forest (Amendment) Act, 2000 and the (draft) Social Forestry Rules, 2000,* Society for Environment and Human Development (SEHD), Dhaka, Bangladesh, May, 2001.

21. Sadeka Halim, "Social Forestry in Bangladesh and the Role of Women" in *Discourse: A Journal of Policy Studies*, Vol. 3, Number 2, Winter, 1999, Institute for Development Policy Analysis and Advocacy, Proshika, Dhaka, pp. 58-79.

22. See, respectively, (i) *Danish Strategy for Indigenous Peoples* and (ii) Working Document of the [European] Commission of May, 1998.

23. Asian Development Bank, *Policy on Indigenous Peoples*, p. 17.

24. *Ibid.*, pp. 13-15.

25. See, for example, statement of representative of Indigenous Peoples' Organisations participating at the Round Table meeting on the World Bank's Indigenous Peoples' Policy in Washington, DC, USA on 17 October 2002.

26. See, e.g., (i) Philip Gain, *The Last Forests of Bangladesh*, Society for Environment and Human Development, Dhaka, February, 1998 (esp. pp. 151-174) and (ii) Suhas Chakma, "ADB Programs in Bangladesh: Identifying the Critical Issues", in *Indigenous Perspectives: A Journal of the Tebtebba Foundation,* Vol. III, Number 1, Baguio City, Philippines, 2000, pp. 140-150.

27. This project was initiated through ADB Loan No. 1771-BAN (SF). The project commenced in May, 2004 and is scheduled for completion in March, 2008. See, e.g., *Project Proforma of the Ministry of Chittagong Hill Tracts Affairs, Government of Bangladesh, March, 2004* and SMEC International Pty Ltd, *Chittagong Hill Tracts Rural Development Project: Second Consultant Report to the CHT Regional Coordination Committee,* 13 July 2005.

28. Project Proforma of the Ministry of Chittagong Hill Tracts Affairs, Government of Bangladesh, March 2004, p. 67 (Annexe 20).

29. SMEC International Pty Ltd, Chittagong Hill Tracts Rural Development Project: Second Consultant Report to the CHT Regional Coordination Committee, 13 July 2005, pp. 7-14.

30. Agreement on Loan No. 1771 BAN (SF) on the *Chittagong Hill Tracts Rural Development Project* between the People's Republic of Bangladesh and the Asian Development Bank, dated, 18 December 2000 (esp. Schedule 6, paragraph 30).

31. Report and Recommendation of the President to the Board of Directors on a Proposed Loan to the People's Republic of Bangladesh for the Chittagong Hill Tracts Rural Development Project (RRP: BAN 32467), Asian Development Bank, October 2000, p. 16 (paragraphs 46, 47).

32. 5th meeting of Regional Coordination Committee of the Chittagong Hill Tracts Rural Development Project, held in Rangamati, Chittagong Hill Tracts, Bangladesh on 4 July, 2005, attended by the writer (in his capacity as a member of the committee by virtue of being one of the chiefs of the region). The local NGO, Taungya, withdrew its application to be included among the local NGOs to help implement the project when it realised that it would have to also engage in a micro credit operation by investing its own funds (in addition to subsidies from the government); interview with Amlan Chakma, Executive Director, Taungya, Rangamati, Bangladesh, 25 October 2005.

33. Asian Development Bank, *Policy on Indigenous Peoples*, p. 24.

34. This comment was made in the presence of this writer, some years ago in an international meeting related to indigenous peoples' rights by a World Bank official, whose identity it would not be rights to divulge without his consent.

35. Statement of Indigenous Participants at the Consultation on the World Bank's Draft Policy on Indigenous Peoples (OP/BP 4.10), Dhaka, Bangladesh, 14 November 2001, attended by this writer.

36. For example, the ADB held one formal consultation with indigenous peoples' representatives regarding its (then daft) *Indigenous Peoples* policy in Punta Baluarte, Philippines in 1995 (which was also attended by this writer).

37. For example, the *Regional Workshop on Review of the Asian Development Bank's Forestry Policy* held in Manila, Philippines, on 14-15 February 2002 (attended by this writer).

38. For example, in the case of the draft Indigenous Peoples' policy meeting held in Punta Baluarte, Philippines, 1995.
39. For example, in the Forestry policy held in Manila on 14-15 February 2002, this writer was perhaps among only one or two participants who criticised the draft policy, with the overwhelming majority of participants remaining either silent or making non-critical remarks about the draft. This writer concluded, therefore, that this was substantively an orchestrated meeting that consciously excluded critical voices. This is also the opinion of Chris Lang in 'ADB's Draft Forest Policy: The Politics of Participation', published in WRM Bulletin 74, September 2003.
40. See, for example, the statement of representative of Indigenous Peoples' Organisations participating at the Round Table meeting on the World Bank's Indigenous Peoples' Policy held in *Washington, DC, USA* on 17 October 2002 (attended by this writer).
41. In its new policy on indigenous peoples (OP 4.10), the World Bank mentioned the requirement of Prior Informed *Consultation*, which has been rejected by indigenous peoples since it falls short of the principle of Prior Informed *Consent*.
42. This writer was among the participants at a formal consultation on the policy held at Punta Baluarte, Philippines, in 1995. Many of the participants at the meeting felt that the process of consultations was not participatory enough and therefore advised the Bank's representatives to hold further formal consultations with indigenous peoples' representatives, which advice does not seem to have been accepted or acted upon by the bank.
43. See for example, Chris Lang in "ADB's Draft Forest Policy: The Politics of Participation", published in WRM Bulletin 74, September 2003.
44. See, for example, the letter written by representatives of indigenous peoples to the Vice Chairman of the World Bank, on 24 March 2004 expressing concern over the process of consultations.
45. Statement of representative of Indigenous Peoples' Organisations participating at a *Round Table* meeting on the World Bank's Indigenous Peoples' Policy held in Washington, DC, USA on 17 October 2002.
46. Suhas Chakma, 'ADB Programs in Bangladesh: Identifying the Critical Issues', in *Indigenous Perspectives*: *A Journal of the Tebtebba Foundation*, Vol. III, Number 1, Baguio City, Philippines, 2000, pp. 140-173, at p. 149.

47. Raja Devasish Roy, "Perspectives of Indigenous Peoples on the Review of the Asian Development Bank's Forest Policy", paper presented at the *Regional Workshop on Review of the Asian Development Bank's Forestry Policy* held in Manila, Philippines, on 14-15 February 2002.
48. *Ibid.* See also, Suhas Chakma, *op. cit.,* p. 148.
49. Asian Development Bank, *Policy on Indigenous Peoples*, p. 25.
50. Statement of representative of Indigenous Peoples' Organisations participating at a *Round Table* meeting on the World Bank's Indigenous Peoples' Policy held in Washington, DC, USA on 17 October 2002.

Bibliography

Papers and Articles

Chakma, Suhas, 2000. "ADB Programs in Bangladesh: Identifying the Critical Issues", in *Indigenous Perspectives: A Journal of the Tebtebba Foundation, Vol. III, Number 1,* Baguio City, Philippines, 2000, pp. 140-173.

Gain, Philip 1998. *The Last Forests of Bangladesh*, Society for Environment and Human Development, Dhaka, February 1998 (esp. pp. 151-174).

Gain, Philip, 2001. *Background and Context to the Forest (Amendment) Act, 2000 and the (draft) Social Forestry Rules, 2000,* Society for Environment and Human Development (SEHD), Dhaka, Bangladesh, May 2001.

Halim, Sadeka, 1999. "Social Forestry in Bangladesh and the Role of Women" in *Discourse: A Journal of Policy Studies*, Vol. 3, Number 2, Winter, 1999, Institute for Development Policy Analysis and Advocacy, Proshika, Dhaka, pp. 58-79.

Lang, Chris, 2003. "ADB's Draft Forest Policy: The Politics of Participation", published in WRM Bulletin 74, September 2003.

Minority Rights Group (ed.), *Forests and Indigenous Peoples of Asia,* Report 98/4, London, 1999.

Roy, Raja Devasish, 2002. "Perspectives of Indigenous Peoples on the Review of the Asian Development Bank's Forest Policy", paper presented at the *Regional Workshop on Review of the Asian Development Bank's Forestry Policy* held in Manila, Philippines, on 14-15 February 2002.

________ and Philip Gain, 1999. *Indigenous Peoples and Forests in Bangladesh* in Minority Rights Group (ed,), *Forests and Indigenous Peoples of Asia,* Report 98/4, London, 1999, pp. 21-22.

________and Sadeka Halim, 2001. "A Critique to the Forest (Amendment) Act of 2000 and (Draft) Social Forestry Rules of 2000", published by Society for Environment and Human Development (SEHD), Dhaka, Bangladesh, May 2001.

Other Documents

Asian Development Bank, 1998. *Policy on Indigenous Peoples,* Manila, Philippines.

_______, 2000. *Report and Recommendation of the President to the Board of Directors on a Proposed Loan to the People's Republic of Bangladesh for the Chittagong Hill Tracts Rural Development Project* (RRP: BAN 32467), Asian Development Bank, October, 2000.

European Commission, 1998. *Working Document of the [European] Commission of May 1998.*

Ministry of Chittagong Hill Tracts Affairs, 2004. Project Proforma for *Chittagong Hill Tracts Rural Development Project,* Ministry of Chittagong Hill Tracts Affairs, Government of Bangladesh, March 2004.

Ministry of Foreign Affairs, Government of Denmark, 1998. *Danish Strategy for Indigenous Peoples*. SMEC International Pty Ltd., 2005.

Chittagong Hill Tracts Rural Development Project: Second Consultant Report to the CHT Regional Coordination Committee, 13 July 2005.

World Bank, Operational Directive 4.20, Operational Policy 4.10, Bank Procedure 4.10.

Part II
United Nations and the Indigenous Peoples

Introduction

Part II deals with the interaction that has been taking place between ILO, the United Nations and the indigenous peoples. In this part, we present two of the conventions – Convention No. 107 and Convention No. 169– of ILO that deal with the indigenous peoples and their issues. We also present the Recommendations 104, concerning the Protection and Integration of Indigenous and Other Tribal and Semi-Tribal Populations in Independent Countries under the initiative of ILO. The fourth selection is the United Nations' Declaration on the Rights of Indigenous Peoples. The fifth and the final selection in this part is about the constitution of the Permanent Forum for Indigenous Peoples. Hence, Part II has been termed, 'United Nations and Indigenous Peoples'.

ILO was created in 1919 by means of the Treaty of Versailles. When the United Nations was established in 1946, ILO was the first specialised agency associated with the UN, with special responsibility for work and social Issues. ILO currently has 175 member States. Thus, ILO has been significantly exceptional among international organisations in addressing issues related to indigenous peoples.

The tasks of ILO include promoting social justice for workers, and formulating international policies and programmes to contribute to improving their living and working conditions. It prepares international labour standards, which serve as guidelines for authorities in implementing these policies, and undertakes training and education programmes in order to contribute to continuing these efforts.

ILO was the first international organisation to take up the indigenous peoples issues. ILO began its work on indigenous peoples in 1930s, when the organisation began to pay particular attention to the situation of the peoples then known as 'Native workers'. This need was recognised very early in 1926 with creation of a Committee of Experts in charge of drawing up international standards for the protection of indigenous and tribal workers, as they were found to be numerous among bonded laboures. The original concern was to protect these workers, as wage earners from exploitive and discriminatory employment practice. But it rapidly became apparent that no lasting solution was achievable unless the needs of the self-employed, marginal farmers, forest-dwelling and nomadic indigenous and tribal people were also addressed.

In 1953, ILO published a study on indigenous peoples and this led in 1957 to the adoption of Convention No. 107 titled, 'Convention Concerning the Protection and Integration of Indigenous and Other Tribal and Semi-Tribal Populations in Independent Countries'. At that time, this was the only international convention on the subject concerning the protection and integration of indigenous peoples and tribal populations. The Convention No. 107 does not merely recognise 'the right of ownership, collective or individual, of the members of the populations concerned over the lands which these populations traditionally occupy'. It also recognises their rights to be compensated in money or in kind for lands appropriated by the national government for development purposes.

It needs to be stated here that the Convention No. 107 reflects the common view of 1940s and 1950s in promoting assimilation or integration and non-discrimination. For instance, Article 27 directs the states to develop agencies to administer the indigenous peoples' areas. Thus, it fails to consider the administrative systems the indigenous peoples have evolved over the years. Similarly, Article 11 only speaks about recognising the land rights of the indigenous peoples and not the protection of it. Further, the basic position of the framers of the convention was assimilationist than ensuring the independence and dignity of the indigenous peoples.

With the changes that were taking place in the world, the Convention 107, though well intended, became out dated and faced lots of criticism. By then, the indigenous peoples and their organisations had come to the public forums and began to speak their mind and demanded for equality, participation and self-determination. Taking these into account, ILO convened a conference in 1989 and came up with Convention 169 with a changed title, "Convention Concerning Indigenous and Tribal Peoples in Independent Countries". This convention came into effect in 1991.

The Convention 169 recognises the fact that in many parts of the world, the indigenous peoples are not able to enjoy their fundamental rights to the same degree as the rest of the population of the states within which they live. It also gives the directives that the indigenous and tribal people shall enjoy the full measure of human rights and fundamental freedoms without hindrance or discrimination. The provisions of the Convention shall be applied without discrimination to male and female members of these people (Article 3). Thus, the language and content of the convention itself is a changed one.

Article 4 directs the states to put in place special measures appropriate for safeguarding the persons, institutions, property, labour, cultures and environment of the peoples concerned. But these special measures shall not be super imposed but based on the freely expressed wishes of the peoples concerned. Again, article 15 directs the states that the rights of the peoples concerned to the natural resources pertaining to their lands shall be specially safeguarded. These rights include the right of these people to participate in the use, management and conservation of these resources. Thus, ownership, access and control over all resources of the indigenous peoples are to be protected and promoted by the states.

From the above, discussion, we gather that the provisions mentioned in Convention 169 as compared to Convention 107, are progressive. It paved the way for making many demands of the indigenous peoples into legal rights. Like the other international instruments, all those countries that ratified the Convention, must send reports to ILO on how it is being implemented. These reports must include information on the situation of indigenous and tribal people, both in legislative and practical terms. But in reality even these well meaning instruments remain unimplemented. It is further depressing that India has not ratified both the 107 and 169 Conventions.

In late 1960s and early 1970s, movements by the indigenous peoples rose in large number of countries in response to the discrimination and exploitation that they were subjected to. Moreover, attempts to assimilate them in 'mainstream' society and systematic violations of their most basic rights led to the uprising of the indigenous peoples. This, in the course of time, led to the self-determination movement of the indigenous peoples. During the course of this struggle, indigenous organisations emerged at the local, national, regional and international level which culminated in the formation of international indigenous lobby. This lobby called upon the international community and, particularly, the human rights bodies of the UN to consider their situation and take appropriate measures to protect their fundamental rights.

These efforts of the indigenous peoples found support from independent experts, research institutions and some non-governmental organisations. Lobbying by these people led to ensuring the discussion on the status of indigenous peoples in the Sub-Commission on Prevention of Discrimination and Protection of Minorities. In 1972, the Economic and Social Council authorised the Sub-Commission on Prevention of Discrimination and Protection of Minorities to undertake a special study on discrimination against indigenous and tribal peoples. The study undertaken by Martinez Cobo begins with a working definition of who indigenous peoples are and considered an extremely wide spectrum of issues, such as indigenous identity, culture, legal systems, health, housing, education, language etc. It concluded with a series of proposals and recommendations.

On 29 June 2006, the United Nations Human Rights Council (UNHRC) adopted the U.N. Declaration on the Rights of Indigenous Peoples. This decision comes as a result of more than twenty years of work by indigenous peoples and the United Nations system. The efforts to draft a specific instrument dealing with the protection of indigenous peoples worldwide date back over two decades. In 1982 the Economic and Social Council (ECOSOC) established the Working Group on Indigenous Populations (WGIP) with the mandate to develop a set of minimum standards that would protect indigenous peoples. WGIP was established as result of a study by José R. Martinez Cobo on the problem of discrimination faced by indigenous peoples throughout the world. The study outlined the oppression, marginalisation and exploitation suffered by indigenous peoples.

WGIP submitted a first draft declaration on the rights of indigenous peoples to the Sub-Commission on the Prevention of Discrimination and Protection of Minorities, which was later approved in 1994. The Draft was sent for consideration to the then UN Commission on Human Rights for further discussion and if it was deemed to be appropriate, to approve the proposed declaration before its submission to ECOSOC and the UN General Assembly.

The process moved very slowly because of concerns expressed by States with regard to some of the core provisions of the draft declaration, namely the right to self-determination of indigenous peoples and the control over natural resources existing on indigenous peoples' traditional lands. The need to accommodate these issues led to the creation, in 1995, of the open-ended inter-sessional working group to consider and elaborate on the 1994 draft declaration with the view that it would be adopted by the General Assembly within the International Decade of the World's Indigenous People (1995-2004). The mandate of the Working Group was extended by the U.N. Commission on Human Rights into the Second International Decade of the World's Indigenous Peoples (2005-2015). The Commission also urged the Working Group to "present for adoption as soon as possible a final draft United Nations declaration on the rights of indigenous people".

At the 11th Session of the Working Group 2005-06, the Chairperson Mr. Luis-Enrique Chavez (Peru) prepared a compilation of proposals submitted and discussed during the 10th session, which formed the basis of negotiations. The Declaration, adopted by the UN Human Rights Council in June 2006 is the exact version proposed by Chairperson Chavez.

The Declaration is a long and complex document with a preamble and 46 articles. The text recognised the wide range of basic human rights and fundamental freedoms of indigenous peoples. Among these are the right to unrestricted self-determination an inalienable collective right to the ownership, use and control of lands, territories and other natural resources [Article 26], their rights in terms of maintaining and developing their own political, religious, cultural and educational institutions along with the protection of their cultural and intellectual property. The Declaration highlights the requirement for prior and informed consultation, participation and consents in activities of any kind that impact on indigenous peoples, their property or territories. It also establishes the requirement for fair and adequate compensation for violation of the rights recognised in the declaration, and establishes guarantees against ethnocide and genocide.

The Declaration also provides for fair and mutually acceptable procedures to resolve conflicts between indigenous peoples and States, including procedures such as negotiations, mediation, arbitration, national courts and international and regional mechanism for denouncing and examining human rights violations [Article 28].

The Declaration notes that the rights mentioned within it form minimum standards for survival and well-being of the world's indigenous peoples. Article 3 of the Declaration is central and fundamental to the entire Declaration. It states, *"Indigenous people have the right of self – determination. By virtue of that right they freely determine their political status and freely pursue their economic, social and cultural development"*. Article 38 calls upon the State to ensure that this right of the indigenous peoples is respected.

The final selection of Part II is about the establishment of the UN Permanent Forum of Indigenous Peoples. Discussions to establish the UN Permanent Forum of Indigenous Peoples began in the late 1980s. In 1993, the United Nations Economic and Social Council for the first time adopted by consensus a resolution establishing a Permanent Forum for Indigenous Issues, a first in the history of the UN and International Policy. Participants at the 1993 World Conference on Human

Rights in Vienna discussed the creation of the Permanent Forum. The Vienna Declaration and Programme of Action recommended that such a forum should be established within the framework of the first United Nations International Decade of the World's Indigenous Peoples (1995-2004).

In June 1995, a workshop was held in Copenhagen, Denmark, to discuss establishing a permanent forum for indigenous peoples. Participants included representatives of governments, indigenous peoples and independent experts. They discussed the potential scope of a permanent forum, which UN body the proposed forum would report to, the forum's mandate and terms of reference, including what activities it might undertake, membership, indigenous participation, its relationship with the Working Group on Indigenous Populations, and financial and secretariat implications. The report of this workshop was transmitted to governments, indigenous peoples' organisations, and inter-governmental and non-governmental organisations. Recipients of the report were invited to express their views.

When the General Assembly adopted the Programme of Activities for the International Decade of the World's Indigenous People, it recognised that the establishment of the Forum was one of the primary objectives of the Decade.

A second UN workshop on the Permanent Forum was held in Santiago, Chile in 1997, during which representatives of governments, indigenous peoples' organisations, NGOs, UN organisations and bodies, and specialised agencies considered the findings of the Secretary-General's review and further developed proposals for establishing a permanent forum.

The Permanent Forum was finally established by the Economic and Social Council in 2000 with a mandate to 'discuss indigenous issues within the mandate of the Council relating to economic and social development, culture, the environment, education, health and human rights'. It comprises 16 independent experts, functioning in their personal capacities. Eight of the members are nominated by Governments and eight directly by indigenous organisations in their respective regions. From the time of its establishment, the Forum has been highlighting the issues of the indigenous peoples.

From 18-29 May 2009, the Permanent Forum met to discuss ways to further implement the Declaration on the Rights of Indigenous Peoples, which gained momentum in 2010, when Australia officially endorsed it after previously having voted against it. Some 2,000 indigenous representatives from all regions of the world participated in the eighth session of the Forum, as representatives of Member States, civil society, academia, some 35 United Nations system bodies and other inter-governmental organisations. The Forum also discussed the relationship between indigenous peoples and industrial corporations, and the need to promote corporate social responsibility. A report submitted to the Forum noted that industries such as mineral, oil and gas extraction disproportionately impact indigenous peoples. Other issues on the Forum's agenda included climate change, the Arctic region and land tenure.

12

International Labour Organisation (ILO) Convention 107

Convention Concerning the Protection and Integration of Indigenous and Other Tribal and Semi-Tribal Populations in Independent Countries

Note:

Convention: C 107
Place: Geneva
Session of the Conference: 40
Date of adoption: 26:06:1957
Date of coming into force: 02:06:1959
This Convention was revised in 1989 by Convention No. 169

The General Conference of the International Labour Organisation

Having been convened at Geneva by the Governing Body of the International Labour Office, and having met in its Fortieth Session on 5 June 1957, and

Having decided upon the adoption of certain proposals with regard to the protection and integration of indigenous and other tribal and semi-tribal populations in independent countries, which is the sixth item on the agenda of the session, and

Having determined that these proposals shall take the form of an international Convention, and

Considering that the Declaration of Philadelphia affirms that all human beings have the right to pursue both their material wellbeing and their spiritual development in conditions of freedom and dignity, of economic security and equal opportunity, and

Considering that there exist in various independent countries indigenous and other tribal and semi-tribal populations which are not yet integrated into the national community and whose social, economic or cultural situation hinders them from benefiting fully from the rights and advantages enjoyed by other elements of the population, and

Considering it desirable both for humanitarian reasons and in the interest of the countries concerned to promote continued action to improve the living and working conditions of these populations by simultaneous action in respect of all the factors which have hitherto prevented them from sharing fully in the progress of the national community of which they form part, and

Considering that the adoption of general international standards on the subject will facilitate action to assure the protection of the populations concerned, their progressive integration into their respective national communities, and the improvement of their living and working conditions, and

Noting that these standards have been framed with the co-operation of the United Nations, the Food and Agriculture Organisation of the United Nations, the United Nations Educational, Scientific and Cultural Organisation and the World Health Organisation, at appropriate levels and in their respective fields, and that it is proposed to seek their continuing co-operation in promoting and securing the application of these standards, adopts this twenty-sixth day of June of the year one thousand nine hundred and fifty-seven the following Convention, which may be cited as the Indigenous and Tribal Populations Convention, 1957:

PART I. GENERAL POLICY

Article I

1. This Convention applies to :

(a) Members of tribal or semi-tribal populations in independent countries whose social and economic conditions are at a less advanced stage than the stage reached by the other sections of the national community, and whose status is regulated wholly or partially by their own customs or traditions or by special laws or regulations:

(b) members of tribal or semi-tribal populations in independent countries which are regarded as indigenous on account of their descent from the populations which inhabited the country, or a geographical region to which the country belongs, at the time of conquest or colonisation and which, irrespective of their legal status, live more in conformity with the social, economic and cultural institutions of that time than with the institutions of the nation to which they belong.

2. For the purposes of this Convention, the term 'semi-tribal' includes groups and persons who, although they are in the process of losing their tribal characteristics are not jet integrated into the national community.

3. The indigenous and other tribal or semi-tribal populations mentioned in paragraphs 1 and 2 of this Article are referred to hereinafter as 'the populations concerned'.

Article 2

1. Governments shall have the primary responsibility for developing coordinated and systematic action for the protection of the populations concerned and their progressive integration into the life of their respective countries.

2. Such action shall include measures for :

(a) enabling the said populations to benefit on an equal footing from the rights and opportunities which national laws or regulations grant to the other elements of the population;

(b) promoting the social, economic and cultural development of these populations and raising their standard of living;

(c) creating possibilities of national integration to the exclusion of measures tending towards the artificial assimilation of these populations,

3. The primary objective of all such action shall be the fostering of individual dignity, and the advancement of individual usefulness and initiative.
4. Recourse to force or coercion as a means of promoting the integration of these populations into the national community shall be excluded.

Article 3

1. So long as the social, economic and cultural conditions of the populations concerned prevent them from enjoying the benefits of the general laws of the country to which they belong, special measures shall be adopted for the protection of the institutions, persons, property and labour of these populations.
2. Care shall be taken to ensure that such special measures of protection :
   (a) are not used as a means of creating or prolonging a state of segregation; and
   (b) will be continued only so long as there is need for special protection and only to the extent that such protection is necessary.
3. Enjoyment of the general rights of citizenship without discrimination, shall not be prejudiced in any way by such special measures of protection.

Article 4

In applying the provisions of this Convention relating to the integration of the populations concerned :

(a) due account shall be taken of the cultural and religious values and of the forms of social control existing among these populations, and of the nature of the problems which face them both as groups and as individuals when they undergo social and economic change;

(b) the danger involved in disrupting the values and institutions of the said populations unless they can be replaced by appropriate substitutes which the groups concerned are willing to accept shall be recognised;

(c) policies aimed at mitigating the difficulties experienced by these populations in adjusting themselves to new conditions of life and work shall be adopted.

Article 5

in applying the provisions of this Convention relating to the protection and integration of the populations concerned, governments shall-

(a) seek the collaboration of these populations and of their representatives;

(b) provide these populations with opportunities for the full development of their initiative;

(c) stimulate by all possible means the development among these populations of civil liberties and the establishment of or participation in elective institutions.

Article 6

The improvement of the conditions of life and work and level of education of the populations concerned shall be given high priority in plans for the over-all economic development of areas inhabited by these populations. Special projects for economic development of the areas in Question shall also be so designed as to promote such improvement.

Article 7

1. In defining the rights and duties of the populations concerned regard shall be had to their customary laws.
2. These populations shall be allowed to retain their own customs and Institutions where these are not incompatible with the national legal system or the objectives of integration programmes.
3. The application of the preceding paragraphs of this Article shall not prevent members of these populations from exercising, according to their individual capacity, the rights granted to all citizens and from assuming the corresponding duties.

Article 8

To the extent consistent with the interests of the national community and with the national legal system of :

(a) the methods of social control practiced by the populations concerned shall be used as far as possible for dealing with crimes or offences committed by members of these populations;

(b) Whereas of such methods of social control is not feasible, the customs of these populations in regard to penal matters shall be borne in mind by the authorities and courts dealing with such cases.

Article 9

Except in cases prescribed by law for all citizens the exaction from the members of the populations concerned of compulsory personal services in any form, whether paid or unpaid, shall be prohibited and punishable by law.

Article 10

1. Persons belonging to the populations concerned shall be specially safeguarded against the improper application of preventive detention and shall be able to take legal proceedings for the effective protection of their fundamental rights.
2. In imposing penalties laid down by general law on members of these populations account shall be taken of the degree of cultural development of the populations concerned.
3. Preference shall be given to methods of rehabilitation rather than confinement in prison.

PART II. LAND

Article 11

The right of ownership, collective or individual, of the members of the populations concerned over the lands which these populations traditionally occupy shall be recognised.

Article 12

1. The populations concerned shall not be removed without

their free consent from their habitual territories except in accordance with national laws and regulations for reasons relating to national security, or in the interest of national economic development or of health of the said populations.

2. When in such cases removal of these populations is necessary as an exceptional measure, they shall be provided with lands of quality at least equal to that of the lands previously occupied by them, suitable to provide for their present needs and future development. In cases where chances of alternative employment exist and where the populations concerned prefer to have compensation in money or in kind, they shall be so compensated under appropriate guarantees.
3. Persons thus removed shall be fully compensated for any resulting loss or injury.

Article 13

1. Procedures for the transmission of rights of ownership and use of land which are established by the customs of the populations concerned shall be respected, within the framework of national laws and regulations, in so far as they satisfy the needs of these populations and do not hinder their economic and social development.
2. Arrangements shall be made to prevent persons who are not members of the populations concerned from taking advantage of these customs or of lack of understanding of the laws on the part of the members of these populations to secure the ownership or use of the lands belonging, to such members.

Article 14

National agrarian programmes shall secure to the populations concerned treatment equivalent to that accorded to other sections of the national community with regard to:

(a) the provision of more land for these populations when they have not the area necessary for providing the essentials of a normal existence, or for any possible increase in their numbers;

(b) the provision of the means required to promote the development of the lands which these populations already possess.

PART III. RECRUITMENT AND CONDITIONS OF EMPLOYMENT

Article 15

1. Each Member shall, within the framework of national laws and regulations, adopt special measures to ensure the effective protection with regard to recruitment and conditional of employment of workers belonging to the populations concerned so long as they are not in a position to enjoy the protection granted by law to workers in general,
2. Each Member shall do everything possible to prevent all discrimination between workers belonging to the populations concerned and other workers, in particular as regards:
   (a) admission to employment, including skilled employment;
   (b) equal remuneration for work of equal value;
   (c) medical and social assistance, the prevention of employment injuries, workmen's compensation industrial hygiene and housing;
   (d) the right of association and freedom for all lawful trade union activities and the right to conclude collective agreements with employers or employer's organisations.

PART IV. VOCATIONAL TRAINING, HANDICRAFTS AND RURAL INDUSTRIES

Article 16

Persons belonging to the populations concerned shall enjoy the same opportunities as other citizens in respect of vocational training facilities.

Article 17

1. Whenever programmes of vocational training of general

application do not meet the special needs of persons belonging to the populations concerned governments shall provide special training facilities for such persons.

2. These special training facilities shall be based on a careful study of the economic environment, stage of cultural development and practical needs of the various occupational groups among the said populations; they shall, in particular, enable the persons concerned to receive the training necessary for occupations for which these populations have traditionally shown aptitude.
3. These special training facilities shall be provided only so long as the stage of cultural development of the populations concerned requires them; with advance of the process of integration they shall be replaced by the facilities provided for other citizens.

Article 18

1. Handicrafts and rural Industries shall be encouraged as factors in the economic development of the populations concerned in a manner which will enable these populations to raise their standard of living and adjust themselves to modern methods of production and marketing.
2. Handicrafts and rural industries shall be developed in a manner which preserves the cultural heritage of these populations and improves their artistic values and particular modes of cultural expression.

PART V. SOCIAL SECURITY AND HEALTH

Article 19

Existing social security schemes shall be extended progressively, where practicable, to cover (a) wage earners belonging to the populations concerned, and (b) other persons belonging to these populations.

Article 20

1. Governments shall assume the responsibility for providing adequate health services for the populations concerned.
2. The organisation of such services shall be based on

systematic studies of the social economic and cultural conditions of the populations concerned.

3. The development of such services shall be coordinated with general measures of social, economic and cultural development.

PART VI. EDUCATION AND MEANS OF COMMUNICATION

Article 21

Measures shall be taken to ensure that members of the populations concerned have the opportunity to acquire education at all levels on an equal footing with the rest of the national community.

Article 22

1. Education programmes for the populations concerned shall be adapted, as regards methods and techniques, to the stage these populations have reached in the process of social, economic and cultural integration into the national community.
2. The formulation of such programmes shall normally be preceded by ethnological surveys.

Article 23

1. Children belonging to the populations concerned shall be taught to read and write in their mother tongue or, where this is not practicable, in the, language most commonly used by the group to which they belong.
2. Provision shall be made for a progressive transition from the mother tongue or the vernacular language to the national language or to one of the official languages of the country.
3. Appropriate measures shall, as far as possible, be taken to preserve the mother tongue or the vernacular language.

Article 24

The imparting of general knowledge and skills that will help children to become integrated into the national community shall be an aim of primary education for the populations concerned.

Article 25

Educational measures shall be taken among other sections of the national community and particularly among those that are in most direct contact with the populations concerned with the object of eliminating prejudices that they may harbour in respect of these populations.

Article 26

1. Governments shall adopt measures, appropriate to the social and cultural characteristics of the populations concerned, to make known to them their rights and duties, especially in regard to labour and social welfare.
2. If necessary this shall be done by means of written translations and through the use of media of mass communication in the languages of these populations.

PART VII. ADMINISTRATION

Article 27

1. The governmental authority responsible for the matters covered in this Convention shall create or develop agencies to administer the programmes involved.
2. These programmes shall include:
   (a) planning, co-ordination and execution of appropriate measures for the social, economic and cultural development of the populations concerned;
   (b) proposing of legislative and other measures to the competent authorities;
   (c) Supervision of the application of these measures.

PART VIII. GENERAL PROVISIONS

Article 28

The nature and the scope of the measures to be taken to give effect to this Convention shall be determined in a flexible manner, having regard to the conditions characteristic of each country.

Article 29

The application of the provisions of this Convention shall not affect benefits conferred on the populations concerned in pursuance of other Conventions and Recommendations.

Article 30

The formal ratifications of this Convention shall be communicated to the Director-General of the International Labour Office for registration.

Article 31

1. This Convention shall be binding only upon those Members of the International Labour Organisation whose ratifications have been registered with the Director-General.
2. It shall come into force twelve months after the date on which the ratifications of two Members have been registered with the Director-General.
3. Thereafter, this Convention shall come into force for any Member twelve months after the date on which its ratification has been registered.

Article 32

1. A Member which has ratified this Convention may denounce it after the expiration of ten years from the date on which the Convention first comes into force, by an act communicated to the Director-General of the International Labour Office for registration. Such denunciation shall not take effect until one year after the date on which it is registered.
2. Each Member which has ratified this Convention and which does not, within the year following the expiration of the period of ten years mentioned in the preceding paragraph, exercise the right of denunciation provided for in this Article, will be bound for another period of ten years and, thereafter, may denounce this Convention at the expiration of each period of ten years under terms provided for in this Article.

Article 33

1. The Director-General of the International Labour Office shall notify all Members of the International Labour Organisation of the registration of all ratifications and denunciations communicated to him by the Members of the Organisation.
2. When notifying the Members of the Organisation of the registration of the second ratification communicated to him, the Director-General shall draw the attention of the Members of the Organisation to the date upon which the Convention will come into force.

Article 34

The Director-General of the International Labour Office shall communicate to the Secretary-General of the United Nations for registration in accordance with Article 102 of the Charter of the United Nations full particulars of all ratification and acts of denunciation registered by him in accordance with the provisions of the preceding Articles.

Article 35

At such times as it may consider necessary the Governing Body of the International Labour Office shall present to the General Conference a report on the working of this Convention and shall examine the desirability of placing on the agenda of the Conference the question of its revision in whole or in part.

Article 36

1. Should the Conference adopt a new Convention revising this Convention in whole or in part, then, unless the new Convention otherwise provides:
   (a) the ratification by a Member of the new revising Convention shall ipso jure involve the immediate denunciation of this Convention, notwithstanding the provisions of Article 32 above, if and when the new revising shall have come into force;
   (b) as from the date when the new revising Convention comes into force this Convention shall cease to be open to ratification by the Members.

2. This Convention shall in any case remain in force in its actual form and content for those Members which have ratified it but have not ratified

Article 37

The English and French versions of the text of this Convention are equally authoritative.

13

International Labour Organisation Convention 169

Convention Concerning Indigenous and Tribal Peoples in Independent Countries

The General Conference of the International Labour Organisation,

Having been convened at Geneva by the Governing Body of the International Labour Office, and having met in its 76th Session on 7 June 1989, and

Noting the international standards contained in the Indigenous and Tribal Populations Convention and Recommendation, 1957, and

Recalling the terms of the Universal Declaration of Human Rights, the International Covenant on Economic, Social and Cultural Rights, the International Covenant on Civil and Political Rights, and the many international instruments on the prevention of discrimination, and

Considering that the developments which have taken place in international law since 1957, as well as developments in the situation of indigenous and tribal peoples in all regions of the world, have made it appropriate to adopt new international standards on the subject with a view to removing the assimilations orientation of the earlier standards, and

Recognising the aspirations of these peoples to exercise control over their own institutions, ways of life and economic development and to maintain and develop their identities, languages and religions, within the framework of the States in which they live, and

Noting that in many parts of the world these peoples are unable to enjoy their fundamental human rights to the same degree as the rest of the population of the states within which they live, and that their laws, values, customs and perspectives have often been eroded, and

Calling attention to the distinctive contributions of indigenous and tribal peoples to the cultural diversity and social and ecological harmony of humankind and to international co-operation and understanding, and

Noting that the following provisions have been framed with the co-operation of the United Nations, the Food and Agriculture Organisation of the United Nations, the United Nations Educational, Scientific and Cultural Organisation and the World Health Organisation, as well as of the Inter-American Indian Institute, at appropriate levels and in. their respective fields, and that it is proposed to continue this co-operation in promoting and securing the application of these provisions, and

Having decided upon the adoption of certain proposals with regard to the partial reviser of the Indigenous and Tribal Populations Convention, 1957 (No. 107), which is the fourth item on the agenda of the session, and

Having determined that these proposals shall take the form of an international Convention revising the Indigenous and Tribal Populations Convention, 1957, adopts the twenty-seventh day of June of the year one thousand nine hundred and eighty-nine, the following Convention, which may be cited as the Indigenous and Tribal Peoples Convention, 1989;

PART I. GENERAL POLICY

Article 1

This Convention applies to:

(a) Tribal peoples in independent countries whose social, cultural and economic conditions distinguish them from other sections of the national community, and whose status is regulated wholly or partially by their own customs or traditions or by special laws or regulations;

(b) Peoples in independent countries who are regarded as indigenous on account of their descent from the populations which inhabited the country, or a geographical region to which the country belongs, at the time of conquest or colonisation or the establishment of present state boundaries and who, irrespective of their legal status, retain some or all of their own social, economic, cultural and political institutions.

(c) Self-identification as indigenous or tribal shall be regarded as a fundamental criterion for determining the groups to which the provisions of this Convention apply.

(d) The use of the term peoples in this Convention shall not be construed as having any implications as regards the rights, which may attach to the term under international law.

Article 2

1. Governments shall have the responsibility for developing, with the participation of the peoples concerned, coordinated and systematic action to protect the rights of these peoples and to guarantee respect for their integrity.

Such action shall include measures for:

(a) Ensuring that members of these peoples benefit on an equal footing from the rights and opportunities which national laws and regulations grant to other members of the population;

(b) Promoting the full realisation of the social, economic and cultural rights of these peoples with respect for their social and cultural identity, their customs and traditions and their institutions;

(c) Assisting the members of the peoples concerned to eliminate socio-economic gaps that may exist between indigenous and other members of the national community, in a manner compatible with their aspirations and ways of life.

Article 3

1. Indigenous and tribal peoples shall enjoy the full measure of human rights and fundamental freedoms without hindrance or discrimination. The provisions of the Convention shall he applied without discrimination to male and female members of these peoples.
2. No form of force or coercion shall be used in violation of the human rights and fundamental freedoms of the peoples concerned, including the rights contained in this Convention.

Article 4

1. Special measures shall be adopted as appropriate for safeguarding the persons, institutions, property, labour, cultures and environment of the peoples concerned.
2. Such special measures shall not be contrary to the freely expressed wishes of the peoples concerned.
3. Enjoyment of the general rights of citizenship, without discrimination, shall not be prejudiced in any way by such special treasures.

Article 5

In applying the provisions of this Convention:

(a) The social, cultural, religious and spiritual values and practices of these peoples shall be recognised and protected, and due account shall be taken of the nature of the problems which face them both as groups and as individuals;

(b) The integrity of the values, practices and institutions of these peoples shall be respected;

(c) Policies aimed at mitigating the difficulties experienced by these peoples in facing new condition; of life and work shall be adopted, with the participation and co-operation of the peoples affected.

Article 6

1. In applying the provisions of this Convention, governments shall:

(a) Consult the peoples concerned, through appropriate procedures and in particular through their representative institutions, whenever consideration; is being given to legislative or administrative measures which may affect them directly;

(b) Establish means by which these peoples can freely participate, at least to the same extent as other sectors of the population, at all levels of decision – making in elective institutions and administrative and other bodies responsible for policies and programmes which concern them;

(c) Establish means for the full development of these peoples' own institutions and initiatives, and in appropriate cases provide the resources necessary for this purpose.

2. The consultations carried out in application of this Convention shall be undertaken, in good faith and in a form appropriate to the circumstances, with the objective of achieving agreement or consent to the proposed measures.

Article 7

1. The peoples concerned shall have the right to decide their own priorities for the process of development as it affects their lives, beliefs, institutions and spiritual well-being and the lands they occupy or otherwise use, and to exercise control, to the extent possible, over their own economic, social and cultural development. In addition, they shall participate in the formulation, implementation and evaluation of plans and programmes for national and regional development, which may affect them directly.

2. The improvement of the conditions of life and work and levels of health and education of the peoples concerned, with their participation and co-operation, shall be a matter of priority in plans for the overall economic development of areas they inhabit. Special projects for development of the areas in question shall also be so designed as to promote such improvement.

3. Governments shall ensure that, whenever appropriate, studies arc carried out, in co-operation with the peoples concerned, to assess the social, spiritual, cultural and environmental impact on them of planned development activities. The results of these studies shall be considered as fundamental criteria for the implementation of these activities.
4. Governments shall take measures, in co-operation with the peoples concerned, to protect and preserve the environment of the territories they inhabit.

Article 8

1. In applying national laws and regulations to the peoples concerned, due regard shall be had to their customs or customary laws.
2. These peoples shall have the right to retain their own customs and institutions, where these are not incompatible with fundamental rights defined by the national legal system and will internationally recognised human rights. Procedures shall be established, whenever necessary to resolve conflicts which may arise in the application of this principle.
3. The application of paragraphs I and 2 of this Article shall not prevent members of the indigenous peoples from exercising the rights granted to all citizens and from assuming the corresponding duties.

Article 9

1. To the extent compatible with the national legal system and internationally recognised human rights, the methods customarily practiced by the peoples concerned for dealing with offences committed by their members shall be respected.
2. The customs of these peoples in regard to penal matters shall be taken into consideration the authorities and courts dealing with such cases.

Article 10

1. In imposing penalties lay down by general law on

members of these peoples account shall be taken of their economic, social and cultural characteristics.

2. Preference shall be given to methods of punishment other than confinement in prison.

Article 11

The exaction from members of the peoples concerned of compulsory personal services in any form, whether paid or unpaid, shall be prohibited and punishable by law, except in case prescribed by law for all citizens.

Article 12

The peoples concerned shall be safeguarded against the abuse of their rights and shall be able to take legal proceedings, either individually or through their representative bodies, for the effective protection of these rights. Measures shall be taken to ensure that members of these peoples can understand and be understood in legal proceedings, where necessary through the provision of interpretation or by other effective means.

PART II. LAND

Article 13

1. In applying the provisions of this Part of the Convention, governments shall respect the special importance for the cultures and spiritual values of the peoples concerned of their relationship with the lands or territories, or both as applicable, which they occupy or otherwise use, and in particular the collective aspects of this relationship.
2. The use of the-term lands in Articles 15 and 16 shall include the concept of territories, which covers the total environment of the areas, which the peoples concerned occupy or otherwise use.

Article 14

1. The rights of ownership and possession of the peoples concerned over the lands, which they traditionally occupy, shall be recognised. In addition, measures shall be taken in appropriate cases to safeguard the right of the peoples concerned to use lands not exclusively occupied by them, but to which they have traditionally had access for their

subsistence and traditional activities. Particular attention shall be paid to the situation of nomadic peoples and shifting cultivators in this respect.

2. Governments shall take steps as necessary to identify the lands, which the peoples concerned traditionally occupy, and to guarantee effective protection of their rights of ownership and possession.
3. Adequate procedures shall be established within the national legal system to resolve land claims by the peoples concerned.

Article 15

1. The rights of the peoples concerned to the natural resources pertaining to their lands shall be specially safeguarded. These rights include the right of these peoples to participate in the use, management and conservation of these resources.
2. In cases in which the State retains the ownership of mineral or sub-surface resources or rights to other resources pertaining to lands, governments shall establish or maintain procedures through which they shall consult these peoples, with a view to ascertaining whether and to what degree their interests would be prejudiced, before undertaking or permitting any programmes for the exploration or exploitation of such resources pertaining to their lands. The peoples concerned shall wherever possible participate in the benefits of such activities, and shall receive fair compensation for any damages, which they may sustain as a result of such activities.

Article 16

1. Subject to the following paragraphs of this Article, the peoples concerned shall not be removed from the lands, which they occupy.
2. Where the relocation of these peoples is considered necessary as an exceptional measure, such relocation shall take place only with their free and informed consent. Where their consent cannot be obtained, such relocation shall take place only following appropriate procedures

established by national laws and regulations, including public inquiries where appropriate, which provide the opportunity for effective representation of the peoples concerned.

3. Whenever possible, these peoples shall have the right to return to their traditional lands, as soon as the grounds for relocation cease to exist.
4. When such return is not possible, as determined by agreement or, in the absence of such agreement, through appropriate procedures, these peoples shall be provided in all possible cases with lands of quality and legal status at least equal to that of the lands previously occupied by them, suitable to provide for their present needs and future development where the peoples concerned express a preference for compensation in money or in kind, they shall be so compensated under appropriate guarantees.
5. Persons thus relocated shall be fully compensated for any resulting loss or injury.

Article 17

1. Procedures established by the peoples concerned for the transmission of land rights among members of these peoples shall be respected.
2. The peoples concerned shall be consulted whenever consideration is being given to their capacity to alienate their lands or otherwise transmit their rights outside their own community.
3. Persons not belonging to these peoples shall be prevented from taking advantage of their customs or of lack of understanding of the laws on the part of their members to secure the ownership, possession or use of land belonging to them.

Article 18

Adequate penalties shall be established by law for unauthorised intrusion upon, or use of, the lands of the peoples concerned, and governments shall take measures to prevent such offences.

Article 19

National agrarian programmes shall secure to the peoples concerned treatment equivalent to that accorded to other sectors of the population with regard to:

(a) The provision of more land for these peoples when they have not the area necessary for providing the essentials of a normal existence, or for any possible increase in their numbers;

(b) The provision of the means required promoting the development of the lands, which these peoples already possess.

PART III. RECRUITMENT AND CONDITIONS OF EMPLOYMENT

Article 20

1. Governments shall, within the framework of national laws and regulations, and in cooperation with the peoples concerned, adopt special measures to ensure the effective protection with regard to recruitment and conditions of employment of workers belonging to these peoples, to the extent that laws applicable to workers do not effectively protect them in general.
2. Governments shall do everything possible to prevent any discrimination between workers belonging to the people concerned and other workers, in particular as regards:
   (a) Admission to employment, including skilled employment, as well as measures for promotion and advancement;
   (b) Equal remuneration for work of equal value;
   (c) Medical and social assistance, occupational safety and health, all social security benefits and any other occupationally related benefits, and housing;
   (d) The right of association and freedom for all lawful trade union activities, and the right to conclude collective agreements with employers or employers' organisations.

3. The measures taken shall include measures to ensure:
   (a) That workers belonging to the peoples concerned, including seasonal, casual and migrant workers in agricultural and other employment, as well as those employed by labour contractors, enjoy the protection afforded by national law and practice to other such workers in the same sectors, and that they are fully informed of their rights under labour legislation and of the means of redress available to them;
   (b) That workers belonging to these peoples are not subjected to working conditions hazardous to their health, in particular through exposure to pesticides or other toxic substances;
   (c) That workers belonging to these peoples are not subjected to coercive recruitment systems, including bonded labour and other forms of debt servitude;
   (d) That workers belonging to these peoples enjoy equal opportunities and equal treatment in employment for men and women, and protection from sexual harassment.
4. Particular attention shall be paid to the establishment of adequate labour inspection services in areas where workers belonging to the peoples concerned undertake wage employment, in order to ensure compliance with the provisions of this Part of this Convention.

PART IV. VOCATIONAL TRAINING, HANDICRAFTS AND RURAL INDUSTRIES

Article 21

Members of the peoples concerned shall enjoy opportunities at least equal to those of other citizens in respect of vocational training measures.

Article 22

1. Measures shall be taken to promote the voluntary participation of members of the peoples concerned in vocational training programmes of general application.

2. Whenever existing programmes of vocational training of general application do not meet the special needs of the peoples concerned, governments shall, with the participation of these peoples, ensure the provision of special training programmes and facilities.
3. Any special training programmes shall be based on the economic environment, social and cultural conditions and practical needs of the peoples concerned. Any studies made in this connection shall be carried out in co-operation with these peoples, who shall be consulted on the organisation and operation of such programmes. Where feasible, these peoples shall progressively assume responsibility for the organisation and operation of such special training programmes, if they so decide.

Article 23

1. Handicrafts, rural and community-based industries, and subsistence economy and traditional activities of the peoples concerned, such as hunting, fishing, trapping and gathering, shall be recognised as important factors in the maintenance of their cultures and in their economic self-reliance and development. Governments shall, with the participation of these people and whenever appropriate, ensure that these activities are strengthened and promoted.
2. Upon the request of the peoples concerned, appropriate technical and financial assistance shall be provided wherever possible, taking into account the traditional technologies and cultural characteristics of these peoples, as well as the importance of sustainable and equitable development.

PART V. SOCIAL SECURITY AND HEALTH

Article 24

Social security schemes shall be extended progressively to cover the peoples concerned, and applied without discrimination against them.

Article 25

1. Governments shall ensure that adequate health services

are made available to the peoples concerned, or shall provide them with resources to allow them to design and deliver such services under their own responsibility and control, so that they may enjoy the highest attainable standard of physical and mental health.

2. Health services shall, to the extent possible, be community-based. These services shall be planned and administered in co-operation with the peoples concerned and take into account their economic, geographic, social and cultural conditions as well as their traditional preventive care, healing practices and medicines.
3. The health care system shall give preference to the training and employment of local community health workers, and focus on primary health care while maintaining strong links with other levels of health care services.
4. The provision of such health services shall be coordinated with other social, economic and cultural measures in the country.

PART VI. EDUCATION AND MEANS OF COMMUNICATION

Article 26

Measures shall be taken to ensure that members of the people concerned have the opportunity to acquire education at all levels on at least an equal footing with the rest of the national community.

Article 27

1. Education programmes and services for the peoples concerned shall be developed and implemented in co-operation with them to address their special needs, and shall incorporate their histories, their knowledge and technologies, their value systems and their further social, economic and cultural aspirations.
2. The competent authority shall ensure the training of members of these peoples and their involvement in the formulation and implementation of education programmes, with a view to the progressive transfer of

responsibility for the conduct of these programmes to these peoples as appropriate.

3. In addition, governments shall recognise the right of these peoples to establish their own educational institutions and facilities, provided that such institutions meet minimum standards established by the competent authority in consultation with these peoples. Appropriate resources shall be provided for this purpose.

Article 28

1. Children belonging to the peoples concerned shall, wherever practicable, be taught to read and write in their own indigenous language or in the language most commonly used by the group to which they belong. When this is not practicable, the competent authorities shall undertake consultations with these peoples with a view to the adoption of measures to achieve this objective.
2. Adequate measures shall be taken to ensure that these peoples have the opportunity to attain fluency in the national language or in one of the official languages of the country.
3. Measures shall be taken to preserve and promote the development and practice of the indigenous languages of the peoples concerned.

Article 29

The imparting of general knowledge and skills that will help children belonging to the peoples concerned to participate fully and on an equal footing in their own community and in the national community shall be an aim of education for these peoples.

Article 30

1. Governments shall adopt measures appropriate to the traditions and cultures of the peoples concerned, to make known to them their rights and duties, especially in regard to labour, economic opportunities, education and health matters, social welfare and their rights deriving from this Convention.

2. If necessary, this shall be done by means of written translations and through the use of mass communications in the languages of these peoples.

Article 31

Educational measures shall be taken among all sections of the national community, and particularly among those that are in most direct contact with the peoples concerned, with the object of eliminating prejudices that they may harbour in respect of these peoples. To this end, efforts shall be made to ensure that history textbooks and other educational materials provide a fair, accurate and informative portrayal of the societies and cultures of these peoples.

PART VII. CONTACTS AND CO-OPERATION ACROSS BORDERS

Article 32

Governments shall take appropriate measures, including by means of international agreements, to facilitate contacts and co-operation between indigenous and tribal peoples across borders, including activities in the economic, social, cultural, spiritual and environmental fields.

PART VIII. ADMINISTRATION

Article 33

1. The governmental authority responsible for the matters covered in this Convention shall ensure that agencies or other appropriate mechanisms exist to administer the programmes affecting the peoples concerned, and shall ensure that they have the means necessary for the proper fulfillment of the functions assigned to them.
2. These programmes shall include:
   - (a) The planning, co-ordination, execution and evaluation, in co-operation with the peoples concerned, of the measures provided for in this Convention;
   - (b) The proposing of legislative and other measures to the competent authorities and supervision of the

application of the measures taken, in co-operation with the peoples concerned.

PART IX. GENERAL PROVISIONS

Article 34

The nature and scope of the measures to be taken to give effect to this Convention shall be determined in a flexible manner, having regard to the conditions characteristic of each country.

Article 35

The application of the provisions of this Convention shall not adversely affect rights and benefits of the peoples concerned pursuant to other conventions and recommendations, international instruments, treaties, or national laws, awards, custom or agreements.

PART X. PROVISIONS

Article 36

This Convention revises the Indigenous and Tribal Populations Convention, 1957.

Article 37

The formal ratifications of this Convention shall be communicated to the Director-General of the International Labour Office for registration.

Article 38

1. This Convention shall be binding only upon those Members of the International Labour Organisation whose ratifications have been registered with the Director-General.
2. II shall come into force twelve months after the date on which the ratifications of two Members have been registered with the Director-General.
3. Thereafter, this Convention shall come into force for any Member twelve months after the date on which its ratification has been registered.

Article 39

1. A Member which has ratified this Convention may denounce it after the expiration often years from the date on which the Convention first comes into force, by an act communicated to the Director-General of the International Labour Office for registration. Such denunciation shall not take effect until one year after the date on which it is registered.
2. Each Member which has ratified this Convention and which does not, within the year following the expiration of the period often years mentioned in the preceding, paragraph, exercise the right of denunciation provided for in this Article, will be bound for another period of ten years and, thereafter, may denounce this Convention at the expiration of each period often years under the terms provided for in this Article.

Article 40

1. The Director-General of the International Labour Office shall notify all Members of the International Labour Organisation of the registration of all ratifications and denunciations communicated to him by the Members of the Organisation.
2. When notifying the Members of the Organisation of the registration of the second ratification communicated to him, the Director-General shall draw the attention of the Members of the Organisation to the date upon which the Convention will come into force.

Article 41

The Director-General of the International Labour Office shall communicate to the Secretary-General of the United Nations for registration in accordance with Article 102 of the Charter of the United Nations full particulars of all ratifications and acts of denunciation registered by him in accordance with the provisions of the preceding Articles.

Article 42

At such times as it may consider necessary the Governing Body of the International Labour Office shall present to the

General Conference a report on the working of this Convention and shall examine the desirability of placing on the agenda of the Conference the question of it's revision in whole or in part.

Article 43

1. Should the Conference adopt a new Convention revising this Convention in whole or in part, then, unless the new Convention otherwise provides:
   (a) The ratification by a Member of the new revising Convention shall ipso jury involve the immediate denunciation of this Convention, notwithstanding the provisions of Article 39 above, if and when the new revising Convention shall have come into force;
   (b) As from the date when the new revising Convention comes into force this Convention shall cease to be open to ratification by the Members.
   (c) This Convention shall in any case remain in force in its actual form and content for those Members, which have ratified it but have not ratified the revising Convention.

Article 44

The English and French versions of the text of this Convention are equally authoritative.

14

United Nations Declaration on the Rights of Indigenous Peoples

Resolution adopted by the General Assembly

[*without reference to a Main Committee (A/61/L.67 and Add.1)*]

61/295. United Nations Declaration on the Rights of Indigenous Peoples

The General Assembly,

Taking note of the recommendation of the Human Rights Council contained in its resolution 1/2 of 29 June 2006,[1] by which the Council adopted the text of the United Nations Declaration on the Rights of Indigenous Peoples,

Recalling its resolution 61/178 of 20 December 2006, by which it decided to defer consideration of and action on the Declaration to allow time for further consultations thereon, and also decided to conclude its consideration before the end of the sixty-first session of the General Assembly,

Adopts the United Nations Declaration on the Rights of Indigenous Peoples as contained in the annex to the present resolution.

107th plenary meeting

13 September 2007

Annex

United Nations Declaration on the Rights of Indigenous Peoples

The General Assembly,

Guided by the purposes and principles of the Charter of the United Nations, and good faith in the fulfilment of the obligations assumed by States in accordance with the Charter,

Affirming that indigenous peoples are equal to all other peoples, while recognising the right of all peoples to be different, to consider themselves different, and to be respected as such,

Affirming also that all peoples contribute to the diversity and richness of civilisations and cultures, which constitute the common heritage of humankind,

Affirming further that all doctrines, policies and practices based on or advocating superiority of peoples or individuals on the basis of national origin or racial, religious, ethnic or cultural differences are racist, scientifically false, legally invalid, morally condemnable and socially unjust,

Reaffirming that indigenous peoples, in the exercise of their rights, should be free from discrimination of any kind,

Concerned that indigenous peoples have suffered from historic injustices as a result of, inter alia, their colonisation and dispossession of their lands, territories and resources, thus preventing them from exercising, in particular, their right to development in accordance with their own needs and interests,

Recognising the urgent need to respect and promote the inherent rights of indigenous peoples which derive from their political, economic and social structures and from their cultures, spiritual traditions, histories and philosophies, especially their rights to their lands, territories and resources,

Recognising also the urgent need to respect and promote the rights of indigenous peoples affirmed in treaties, agreements and other constructive arrangements with States,

Welcoming the fact that indigenous peoples are organising themselves for political, economic, social and cultural enhancement and in order to bring to an end all forms of discrimination and oppression wherever they occur,

Convinced that control by indigenous peoples over developments affecting them and their lands, territories and resources will enable them to maintain and strengthen their institutions, cultures and traditions, and to promote their development in accordance with their aspirations and needs,

Recognising that respect for indigenous knowledge, cultures and traditional practices contributes to sustainable and equitable development and proper management of the environment,

Emphasising the contribution of the demilitarisation of the lands and territories of indigenous peoples to peace, economic and social among nations and peoples of the world,

Recognising in particular the right of indigenous families and communities to retain shared responsibility for the upbringing, training, education and well-being of their children, consistent with the rights of the child,

Considering that the rights affirmed in treaties, agreements and other constructive arrangements between States and indigenous peoples are, in some situations, matters of international concern, interest, responsibility and character,

Considering also that treaties, agreements and other constructive arrangements, and the relationship they represent, are the basis for a strengthened partnership between indigenous peoples and States,

Acknowledging that the Charter of the United Nations, the International Covenant on Economic, Social and Cultural Rights[2] and the International Covenant on Civil and Political Rights, as well as the Vienna Declaration and Programme of Action,[3] affirm the fundamental importance of the right to self-determination of all peoples, by virtue of which they freely determine their political status and freely pursue their economic, social and cultural development,

Bearing in mind that nothing in this Declaration may be used to deny any peoples their right to self-determination, exercised in conformity with international law,

Convinced that the recognition of the rights of indigenous peoples in this Declaration will enhance harmonious and cooperative relations between the State and indigenous peoples, based on principles of justice, democracy, respect for human rights, non-discrimination and good faith,

Encouraging States to comply with and effectively implement all their obligations as they apply to indigenous peoples under international instruments, in particular those related to human rights, in consultation and cooperation with the peoples concerned,

Emphasising that the United Nations has an important and continuing role to play in promoting and protecting the rights of indigenous peoples,

Believing that this Declaration is a further important step forward for the recognition, promotion and protection of the rights and freedoms of indigenous peoples and in the development of relevant activities of the United Nations system in this field,

Recognising and reaffirming that indigenous individuals are entitled without discrimination to all human rights recognised in international law, and that indigenous peoples possess collective rights which are indispensable for their existence, well-being and integral development as peoples,

Recognising that the situation of indigenous peoples varies from region to region and from country to country and that the significance of national and regional particularities and various historical and cultural backgrounds should be taken into consideration,

Solemnly proclaims the following United Nations Declaration on the Rights of Indigenous Peoples as a standard of achievement to be pursued in a spirit of partnership and mutual respect:

Article 1

Indigenous peoples have the right to the full enjoyment, as a collective or as individuals, of all human rights and fundamental freedoms as recognised in the Charter of the United Nations, the Universal Declaration of Human Rights and international human rights law.

Article 2

Indigenous peoples and individuals are free and equal to all other peoples and individuals and have the right to be free from any kind of discrimination, in the exercise of their rights, in particular that based on their indigenous origin or identity.

Article 3

Indigenous peoples have the right to self-determination. By virtue of that right they freely determine their political status and freely pursue their economic, social and cultural development.

Article 4

Indigenous peoples, in exercising their right to self-determination, have the right to autonomy or self-government in matters relating to 4.Resolution 217 A (III).

Their internal and local affairs, as well as ways and means for financing their autonomous functions.

Article 5

Indigenous peoples have the right to maintain and strengthen their distinct political, legal, economic, social and cultural institutions, while retaining their right to participate fully, if they so choose, in the political, economic, social and cultural life of the State.

Article 6

Every indigenous individual has the right to a nationality.

Article 7

1. Indigenous individuals have the rights to life, physical and mental integrity, liberty and security of person.
2. Indigenous peoples have the collective right to live in freedom, peace and security as distinct peoples and shall not be subjected to any act of genocide or any other act of violence, including forcibly removing children of the group to another group.

Article 8

1. Indigenous peoples and individuals have the right not to be subjected to forced assimilation or destruction of their culture.

2. States shall provide effective mechanisms for prevention of, and redress for:
   (*a*) Any action which has the aim or effect of depriving them of their integrity as distinct peoples, or of their cultural values or ethnic identities;
   (*b*) Any action which has the aim or effect of dispossessing them of their lands, territories or resources;
   (*c*) Any form of forced population transfer which has the aim or effect of violating or undermining any of their rights;
   (*d*) Any form of forced assimilation or integration;
   (*e*) Any form of propaganda designed to promote or incite racial or ethnic discrimination directed against them.

Article 9

Indigenous peoples and individuals have the right to belong to an indigenous community or nation, in accordance with the traditions and customs of the community or nation concerned. No discrimination of any kind may arise from the exercise of such a right.

Article 10

Indigenous peoples shall not be forcibly removed from their lands or territories. No relocation shall take place without the free, prior and informed consent of the indigenous peoples concerned and after agreement on just and fair compensation and, where possible, with the option of return.

Article 11

1. Indigenous peoples have the right to practise and revitalise their cultural traditions and customs. This includes the right to maintain, protect and develop the past, present and future manifestations of their cultures, such as archaeological and historical sites, artefacts, designs, ceremonies, technologies and visual and performing arts and literature.

2. States shall provide redress through effective mechanisms, which may include restitution, developed in conjunction with indigenous peoples, with respect to their cultural, intellectual, religious and spiritual property taken without their free, prior and informed consent or in violation of their laws, traditions and customs.

Article 12

1. Indigenous peoples have the right to manifest, practise, develop and teach their spiritual and religious traditions, customs and ceremonies; the right to maintain, protect, and have access in privacy to their religious and cultural sites; the right to the use and control of their ceremonial objects; and the right to the repatriation of their human remains.
2. States shall seek to enable the access and/or repatriation of ceremonial objects and human remains in their possession through fair, transparent and effective mechanisms developed in conjunction with indigenous peoples concerned.

Article 13

1. Indigenous peoples have the right to revitalise, use, develop and transmit to future generations their histories, languages, oral traditions, philosophies, writing systems and literatures, and to designate and retain their own names for communities, places and persons.
2. States shall take effective measures to ensure that this right is protected and also to ensure that indigenous peoples can understand and be understood in political, legal and administrative proceedings, where necessary through the provision of interpretation or by other appropriate means.

Article 14

1. Indigenous peoples have the right to establish and control their educational systems and institutions providing education in their own languages, in a manner appropriate to their cultural methods of teaching and learning.

2. Indigenous individuals, particularly children, have the right to all levels and forms of education of the State without discrimination.
3. States shall, in conjunction with indigenous peoples, take effective measures, in order for indigenous individuals, particularly children, including those living outside their communities, to have access when possible, to an education in their own culture and provided in their own language.

Article 15

1. Indigenous peoples have the right to the dignity and diversity of their cultures, traditions, histories and aspirations which shall be appropriately reflected in education and public information.
2. States shall take effective measures, in consultation and cooperation with the indigenous peoples concerned, to combat prejudice and eliminate discrimination and to promote tolerance, understanding and good relations among indigenous peoples and all other segments of society.

Article 16

1. Indigenous peoples have the right to establish their own media in their own languages, and to have access to all forms of non-indigenous media without discrimination.
2. States shall take effective measures to ensure that State-owned media duly reflect indigenous cultural diversity. States, without prejudice to ensuring full freedom of expression, should encourage privately owned media to adequately reflect indigenous cultural diversity.

Article 17

1. Indigenous individuals and peoples have the right to enjoy fully all rights established under applicable international and domestic labour law.
2. States shall in consultation and cooperation with indigenous peoples take specific measures to protect indigenous children from economic exploitation and from performing any work that is likely to be hazardous or to

interfere with the child's education, or to be harmful to the child's health or physical, mental, spiritual, moral or social development, taking into account their special vulnerability and the importance of education for their empowerment.

3. Indigenous individuals have the right not to be subjected to any discriminatory conditions of labour and, *inter alia*, employment or salary.

Article 18

Indigenous peoples have the right to participate in decision-making in matters which would affect their rights, through representatives chosen by themselves in accordance with their own procedures, as well as to maintain and develop their own indigenous decision making institutions.

Article 19

States shall consult and cooperate in good faith with the indigenous peoples concerned through their own representative institutions in order to obtain their free, prior and informed consent before adopting and implementing legislative or administrative measures that may affect them.

Article 20

1. Indigenous peoples have the right to maintain and develop their political, economic and social systems or institutions, to be secure in the enjoyment of their own means of subsistence and development, and to engage freely in all their traditional and other economic activities.
2. Indigenous peoples deprived of their means of subsistence and development are entitled to just and fair redress.

Article 21

1. Indigenous peoples have the right, without discrimination, to the improvement of their economic and social conditions, including, inter alia, in the areas of education, employment, vocational training and retraining, housing, sanitation, health and social security.
2. States shall take effective measures and, where appropriate, special measures to ensure continuing

improvement of their economic and social conditions. Particular attention shall be paid to the rights and special needs of indigenous elders, women, youth, children and persons with disabilities.

Article 22

1. Particular attention shall be paid to the rights and special needs of indigenous elders, women, youth, children and persons with disabilities in the implementation of this Declaration.
2. States shall take measures, in conjunction with indigenous peoples, to ensure that indigenous women and children enjoy the full protection and guarantees against all forms of violence and discrimination.

Article 23

Indigenous peoples have the right to determine and develop priorities and strategies for exercising their right to development. In particular, indigenous peoples have the right to be actively involved in developing and determining health, housing and other economic and social programmes affecting them and, as far as possible, to administer such programmes through their own institutions.

Article 24

1. Indigenous peoples have the right to their traditional medicines and to maintain their health practices, including the conservation of their vital medicinal plants, animals and minerals. Indigenous individuals also have the right to access, without any discrimination, to all social and health services.
2. Indigenous individuals have an equal right to the enjoyment of the highest attainable standard of physical and mental health. States shall take the necessary steps with a view to achieving progressively the full realisation of this right.

Article 25

Indigenous peoples have the right to maintain and strengthen their distinctive spiritual relationship with their traditionally owned or otherwise occupied and used lands, territories, waters and coastal seas and other resources and to uphold their responsibilities to future generations in this regard.

Article 26

1. Indigenous peoples have the right to the lands, territories and resources which they have traditionally owned, occupied or otherwise used or acquired.
2. Indigenous peoples have the right to own, use, develop and control the lands, territories and resources that they possess by reason of traditional ownership or other traditional occupation or use, as well as those which they have otherwise acquired.
3. States shall give legal recognition and protection to these lands, territories and resources. Such recognition shall be conducted with due respect to the customs, traditions and land tenure systems of the indigenous peoples concerned.

Article 27

States shall establish and implement, in conjunction with indigenous peoples concerned, a fair, independent, impartial, open and transparent process, giving due recognition to indigenous peoples' laws, traditions, customs and land tenure systems, to recognise and adjudicate the rights of indigenous peoples pertaining to their lands, territories and resources, including those which were traditionally owned or otherwise occupied or used. Indigenous peoples shall have the right to participate in this process.

Article 28

1. Indigenous peoples have the right to redress, by means that can include restitution or, when this is not possible, just, fair and equitable compensation, for the lands, territories and resources which they have traditionally owned or otherwise occupied or used, and which have been confiscated, taken, occupied, used or damaged without their free, prior and informed consent.

2. Unless otherwise freely agreed upon by the peoples concerned, compensation shall take the form of lands, territories and resources equal in quality, size and legal status or of monetary compensation or other appropriate redress.

Article 29

1. Indigenous peoples have the right to the conservation and protection of the environment, and the productive capacity of their lands or territories and resources. States shall establish and implement assistance programmes for indigenous peoples for such conservation and protection, without discrimination.
2. States shall take effective measures to ensure that no storage or disposal of hazardous materials shall take place in the lands or territories of indigenous peoples without their free, prior and informed consent.
3. States shall also take effective measures to ensure, as needed, that programmes for monitoring, maintaining and restoring the health of indigenous peoples, as developed and implemented by the peoples affected by such materials, are duly implemented.

Article 30

1. Military activities shall not take place in the lands or territories of indigenous peoples, unless justified by a relevant public interest or otherwise freely agreed with or requested by the indigenous peoples concerned.
2. States shall undertake effective consultations with the indigenous peoples concerned, through appropriate procedures and in particular through their representative institutions, prior to using their lands or territories for military activities.

Article 31

1. Indigenous peoples have the right to maintain, control, protect and develop their cultural heritage, traditional knowledge and traditional cultural expressions, as well as the manifestations of their sciences, technologies and cultures, including human and genetic resources, seeds,

medicines, knowledge of the properties of fauna and flora, oral traditions, literatures, designs, sports and traditional games and visual and performing arts. They also have the right to maintain, control, protect and develop their intellectual property over such cultural heritage, traditional knowledge, and traditional cultural expressions.

2. In conjunction with indigenous peoples, States shall take effective measures to recognise and protect the exercise of these rights.

Article 32

1. Indigenous peoples have the right to determine and develop priorities and strategies for the development or use of their lands or territories and other resources.
2. States shall consult and cooperate in good faith with the indigenous peoples concerned through their own representative institutions in order to obtain their free and informed consent prior to the approval of any project affecting their lands or territories and other resources, particularly in connection with the development, utilisation or exploitation of mineral, water or other resources.
3. States shall provide effective mechanisms for just and fair redress for any such activities, and appropriate measures shall be taken to mitigate adverse environmental, economic, social, cultural or spiritual impact.

Article 33

1. Indigenous peoples have the right to determine their own identity or membership in accordance with their customs and traditions. This does not impair the right of indigenous individuals to obtain citizenship of the States in which they live.
2. Indigenous peoples have the right to determine the structures and to select the membership of their institutions in accordance with their own procedures.

Article 34

Indigenous peoples have the right to promote, develop and maintain their institutional structures and their distinctive customs, spirituality, traditions, procedures, practices and, in the cases where they exist, juridical systems or customs, in accordance with international human rights standards.

Article 35

Indigenous peoples have the right to determine the responsibilities of individuals to their communities.

Article 36

1. Indigenous peoples, in particular those divided by international borders, have the right to maintain and develop contacts, relations and cooperation, including activities for spiritual, cultural, political, economic and social purposes, with their own members as well as other peoples across borders.
2. States, in consultation and cooperation with indigenous peoples, shall take effective measures to facilitate the exercise and ensure the implementation of this right.

Article 37

1. Indigenous peoples have the right to recognition, observance and enforcement of treaties, agreements and other constructive arrangements concluded with States or their successors and to have States honour and respect such treaties, agreements and other constructive arrangements.
2. Nothing in this Declaration may be interpreted as diminishing or eliminating the rights of indigenous peoples contained in treaties, agreements and other constructive arrangements.

Article 38

States, in consultation and cooperation with indigenous peoples, shall take the appropriate measures, including legislative measures, to achieve the ends of this Declaration.

Article 39

Indigenous peoples have the right to have access to financial and technical assistance from States and through international cooperation, for the enjoyment of the rights contained in this Declaration.

Article 40

Indigenous peoples have the right to access to and prompt decision through just and fair procedures for the resolution of conflicts and disputes with States or other parties, as well as to effective remedies for all infringements of their individual and collective rights. Such a decision shall give due consideration to the customs, traditions, rules and legal systems of the indigenous peoples concerned and international human rights.

Article 41

The organs and specialised agencies of the United Nations system and other inter-governmental organisations shall contribute to the full realisation of the provisions of this Declaration through the mobilisation, inter alia, of financial cooperation and technical assistance. Ways and means of ensuring participation of indigenous peoples on issues affecting them shall be established.

Article 42

The United Nations, its bodies, including the Permanent Forum on Indigenous Issues, and specialised agencies, including at the country level, and States shall promote respect for and full application of the provisions of this Declaration and follow up the effectiveness of this Declaration.

Article 43

The rights recognised herein constitute the minimum standards for the survival, dignity and well-being of the indigenous peoples of the world.

Article 44

All the rights and freedoms recognised herein are equally guaranteed to male and female indigenous individuals.

Article 45

Nothing in this Declaration may be construed as diminishing or extinguishing the rights indigenous peoples have now or may acquire in the future.

Article 46

1. Nothing in this Declaration may be interpreted as implying for any State, people, group or person any right to engage in any activity or to perform any act contrary to the Charter of the United Nations or construed as authorising or encouraging any action which would dismember or impair, totally or in part, the territorial integrity or political unity of sovereign and independent States.
2. In the exercise of the rights enunciated in the present Declaration, human rights and fundamental freedoms of all shall be respected. The exercise of the rights set forth in this Declaration shall be subject only to such limitations as are determined by law and in accordance with international human rights obligations. Any such limitations shall be non-discriminatory and strictly necessary solely for the purpose of securing due recognition and respect for the rights and freedoms of others and for meeting the just and most compelling requirements of a democratic society.
3. The provisions set forth in this Declaration shall be interpreted in accordance with the principles of justice, democracy, respect for human rights, equality, non-discrimination, good governance and good faith.

Notes

1. See *Official Records of the General Assembly, Sixty-first Session, Supplement No. 53* (A/61/53), part one, chap. II, sect. A.
2. See resolution 2200 A (XXI), annex.
3. A/CONF.157/24 (Part I), chap. III.

15

Establishment of a Permanent Forum on Indigenous Issues

Establishment of a Permanent Forum on Indigenous Issues Economic and Social Council Resolution 2000/22

The Economic and Social Council,

Recalling the provision contained in the final document of the World Conference on Human Rights, held in Vienna in June 1993, according to which the establishment of a permanent forum for indigenous people within the United Nations system should be considered, A/CONF.157/24, (Part I), chap. III, sect. II.B, para. 32.

Recalling also that consideration of the establishment of a permanent forum is recognised as one of the important objectives of the programme of activities for the International Decade of the World's Indigenous People, General Assembly resolution 50/157, annex.

Noting the two workshops on the subject held under the auspices of the Commission on Human Rights in Copenhagen in 1995 and in Santiago in 1997, See E/CN.4/Sub.2/AC.4/1995/7 and E/CN.4/1998/11 and Add.1-3.

Recalling the report of the Secretary-General entitled "Review of the existing mechanisms, procedures, and programmes within the United Nations concerning indigenous people", A/51/493, and noting in particular the striking absence of a mechanism to ensure coordination and regular exchange of information among interested parties — Governments, the United Nations and indigenous people — on an ongoing basis,

Taking into account the deliberations of the Working Group on a permanent forum for indigenous people, See E/CN.4/1999/83 and E/CN.4/2000/86. established pursuant to Commission on Human Rights resolutions 1998/20 of 9 April 1998 See *Official Records of the Economic and Social Council, 1998, Supplement No. 3* (E/1998/23), chap. II, sect. A. and 1999/52 of 27 April 1999 Ibid., *1999, Supplement No. 3* (E/1999/23), chap. II, sect. A. to consider the establishment of a permanent forum and to submit concrete proposals to that effect, as well as the consideration given to the subject at the fifty-sixth session of the Commission,

Wishing to finalise this project during the International Decade of the World's Indigenous People as one means of furthering the objectives of the Decade in partnership between Governments and indigenous people,

Stressing that the establishment of the permanent forum should lead to careful consideration of the future of the Working Group on Indigenous Populations of the Subcommission on the Promotion and Protection of Human Rights,

Bearing in mind the common resolve to promote peace and prosperity in accordance with the Charter of the United Nations, and recalling the functions and powers of the Council in that respect as contained in in the charter,

1. *Decides* to establish as a subsidiary organ of the Council a permanent forum on indigenous issues, consisting of sixteen members, eight members to be nominated by Governments and elected by the Council, and eight members to be appointed by the President of the Council following formal consultation with the Bureau and the regional groups through their coordinators, on the basis of broad consultations with indigenous organisations, taking into account the diversity and geographical distribution of the indigenous people of the world as well as the principles of transparency, representativity and equal opportunity for all indigenous people, including internal processes, when appropriate, and local indigenous consultation processes, with all members serving in their

personal capacity as independent experts on indigenous issues for a period of three years with the possibility of re-election or reappointment for one further period; States, United Nations bodies and organs, intergovernmental organisations and non-governmental organisations in consultative status with the Council may participate as observers; organisations of indigenous people may equally participate as observers in accordance with the procedures which have been applied in the Working Group on Indigenous Populations of the Subcommission on the Promotion and Protection of Human Rights;

2. *Also decides* that the Permanent Forum on Indigenous Issues shall serve as an advisory body to the Council with a mandate to discuss indigenous issues within the mandate of the Council relating to economic and social development, culture, the environment, education, health and human rights; in so doing the Permanent Forum shall:
   (a) Provide expert advice and recommendations on indigenous issues to the Council, as well as to programmes, funds and agencies of the United Nations, through the Council;
   (b) Raise awareness and promote the integration and coordination of activities relating to indigenous issues within the United Nations system;
   (c) Prepare and disseminate information on indigenous issues;
3. *Further decides* that the Permanent Forum shall apply the rules of procedure established for subsidiary organs of the Council as applicable, unless otherwise decided by the Council; the principle of consensus shall govern the work of the Permanent Forum;
4. *Decides* that the Permanent Forum shall hold an annual session of ten working days at the United Nations Office at Geneva or at United Nations Headquarters or at such other place as the Permanent Forum may decide in accordance with existing financial rules and regulations of the United Nations;

5. *Also decides* that the Permanent Forum shall submit an annual report to the Council on its activities, including any recommendations for approval; the report shall be distributed to the relevant United Nations organs, funds, programmes and agencies as a means, *inter alia*, of furthering the dialogue on indigenous issues within the United Nations system;
6. *Further decides* that the financing of the Permanent Forum shall be provided from within existing resources through the regular budget of the United Nations and its specialised agencies and through such voluntary contributions as may be donated;
7. *Decides* that, five years after its establishment, an evaluation of the functioning of the Permanent Forum, including the method for selection of its members, shall be carried out by the Council in the light of the experience gained;
8. *Also decides*, once the Permanent Forum has been established and has held its first annual session, to review, without prejudging any outcome, all existing mechanisms, procedures and programmes within the United Nations concerning indigenous issues, including the Working Group on Indigenous Populations, with a view to rationalising activities, avoiding duplication and overlap and promoting effectiveness.

45th Plenary Meeting

28 July 2000

Part III
International Financial Institutions and the Indigenous Peoples

Introduction

This part deals with the interaction between the international financial institutions and the indigenous peoples. The first selection is the World Bank Policy on Indigenous Peoples. As stated in the document these policies were prepared for use by World Bank staff and are not necessarily a complete treatment of the subject. It was brought out in the year 2005. The second document is the Asian Development Bank's policy on indigenous peoples.

The World Bank states that it aims to promote Indigenous Peoples' development in a manner which ensures that the development process fosters full respect for the dignity, human rights, and uniqueness of Indigenous Peoples. But the impact of the World Bank's projects and programmes on indigenous peoples has been the subject of controversy in recent decades. The structural adjustment programmes promoted by the Bank have been strongly criticised by indigenous peoples and others because they did not take into account the social cost and their impact on the indigenous peoples.

In response to severe international criticism of the destructive impact of its projects on indigenous peoples during the 1960s and 70s, the World Bank adopted its first policy on indigenous peoples in 1982, known as Operational Manual Statement 2.34 (OMS 2.34). This policy requires World Bank staff to include measures to protect the territorial rights, health and cultural integrity of indigenous and to ensure that those peoples affected by projects participate in their planning and implementation. However, in practice, the policy made little contribution to reform within the Bank. The Bank's projects therefore continued to have serious negative impacts on indigenous peoples throughout the 1980s.

For this reason, and to improve implementation of their policies on indigenous peoples, in 1991 the World Bank revised its policy on Indigenous Peoples and produced Operational Directive 4.20 (OD4.20)

This Operational Directive attempts to ensure that Bank staff takes positive action to protect indigenous peoples' rights, guaranteeing land ownership and rights to resources, mitigating the negative impacts of development projects, guaranteeing their participation, and ensuring they share in the benefits. Importantly policy contains provisions for the rejection of projects whose negative impacts cannot be adequately improved or whose borrowers have not presented appropriate plans in terms of complying with the policy.

In spite of weaknesses in this Operational Directive, indigenous peoples consider that this policy could help safeguard the rights of indigenous communities affected by World Bank projects, provided that it is adequately implemented.

During the mid 1990s, Bank began a further review of OD4.20 and other protection policies as part of a 'conversion] process at all levels of the Bank, with the aim of standing and clarifying operational directives for staff and borrowers. According to the Bank, this review was necessary to improve the quality of fulfillment of protection provision. For their part, indigenous peoples expressed a fear that the true reason was to minimise the obligatory rules and limit the cover of the political provisions, and they stated that any new policy should strengthen the existing one, particularly with regard to its provision on land resource security.

In 2000, the Bank published the preliminary policy documents. In spite of the Bank's declarations that there had been no dilution of the regulations with regard to OD4.20, indigenous peoples and NGOs stated that this document was weaker than existing policy, primarily because it contained no obligatory provisions to protect indigenous peoples' land rights; it did not recognise the right to prior and informed consent, it did not prohibit forced resettlement, it lacked indigenous monitoring and supervision requirements of the Bank's operations and it had not been extended to cover structural adjustment loans.

The 2005 document presented here claims and assures, *"This policy contributes to the Bank's mission of poverty reduction and sustainable development by ensuring that the development process fully respects the dignity, human rights, economies, and cultures of Indigenous Peoples. For all projects that are proposed for Bank financing and affect Indigenous Peoples, the Bank requires the borrower to engage in a process of free, prior, and informed consultation."* By free, prior, and informed consultation what is meant is consultation that occurs freely and voluntarily, without any external manipulation, interference, or coercion, for which the parties consulted have prior access to information on the intent and scope of the proposed project in a culturally appropriate manner, form, and language. Further, the record of the consultation is maintained as part of the project file.

It is hoped that the World Bank Guidelines which is under preparation by the World Bank would provide better guidelines for the projects that are to be initiated in the regions where the indigenous people are.

Asian Development Bank (ADB) one of the most powerful international financial institutions in Asia also has come out with policies relating to the indigenous peoples. In 1998, the Bank approved its Policy on Indigenous Peoples. From its document Bank's Policy on Indigenous Peoples, it appears that the Bank is aware of the exploitation the indigenous peoples are subjected to. The 1998 document says, *"Indigenous peoples can be regarded as one of the largest vulnerable segments of society. While differing significantly in terms of culture, identity, economic systems, and social institutions, indigenous peoples as a whole most often reflect specific disadvantage in terms of social indicators, economic status, and quality of life"*.

Recognising the real and potential vulnerability of indigenous peoples in development processes, the policy requires that for development interventions it supports or assists, the Bank will ensure that affected indigenous peoples are at least as well off as they would have been in the absence of the intervention, or that adequate and appropriate compensation is provided. The policy works to ensure the quality of opportunity for indigenous peoples, and that interventions affecting them are (i) consistent with the needs and aspirations of affected peoples; (ii) compatible in substance and structure with affected peoples' cultural, social, and economic institutions, and (iii) conceived, planned, and implemented with the informed participation of affected communities.

The policy on indigenous peoples was developed in close consultation with representatives of indigenous peoples' communities. If an intervention has a negative impact on indigenous peoples, an indigenous peoples plan must be prepared. This plan would address issues and concerns related to affected populations and, as appropriate, would examine measures to avoid or mitigate negative effects, or outline compensation and assistance to be provided when negative effects cannot be avoided. The indigenous peoples. plan would become an integral part of the intervention's design and would include specific provisions to measure success in implementation as well as in delivery of benefits.

Policies worked out by ADB in 1998 are: Anticorruption Policy, Cooperation Between the Asian Development Bank and Non-government Organisations, Graduation Policy, Policy on Gender and Development, and Policy on Indigenous Peoples.

In its recent policy formulations, ADB appears to be more conscious of the need to have caution in issues related to the indigenous peoples. For example, the Poverty Reduction Strategy recognises that the indigenous peoples have special social development needs such as special education curricula, self-managed health care, and other services. Part of the strategy includes investing in social support programmes and a policy reform agenda that promotes equity and empowerment especially for women and disadvantaged groups. ADB extends technical assistance on IP capacity building and policy enhancement to developing member countries.

We already saw in Part I, Raja Devasish Roy, the Chief of the Chakma Administrative Circle in the Chittagong Hill Tracts (CHT), Bangladesh, argued that despite provisions supporting the informed participation of indigenous peoples in ADB-funded interventions, that is, Indigenous Peoples and Forestry Policies, indigenous peoples have not been consulted, substantively, or at all, before and during the formulation and implementation of policies and programmes in the forestry sector in many countries of the Asia-Pacific region, especially in areas that are categorised as forests. Irrespective of all good intensions, the aforesaid interventions have led to many adverse consequences for indigenous peoples.

16

World Bank Policy on Indigenous Peoples

These policies were prepared for use by World Bank staff and are not necessarily a complete treatment of the subject.

OP 4.10 July, 2005

1. This policy[1] contributes to the Bank's[2] mission of poverty reduction and sustainable development by ensuring that the development process fully respects the dignity, human rights, economies, and cultures of Indigenous Peoples. For all projects that are proposed for Bank financing and affect Indigenous Peoples,[3] the Bank requires the borrower to engage in a process of free, prior, and informed consultation.[4] The Bank provides project financing only where free, prior, and informed consultation results in broad community support to the project by the affected Indigenous Peoples.[5] Such Bank-financed projects include measures to (a) avoid potentially adverse effects on the Indigenous Peoples' communities; or (b) when avoidance is not feasible, minimise, mitigate, or compensate for such effects. Bank-financed projects are also designed to ensure that the Indigenous Peoples receive social and economic benefits that are culturally appropriate and gender and inter-generationally inclusive.

2. The Bank recognises that the identities and cultures of Indigenous Peoples are inextricably linked to the lands on which they live and the natural resources on which they depend. These distinct circumstances expose

Indigenous Peoples to different types of risks and levels of impacts from development projects, including loss of identity, culture, and customary livelihoods, as well as exposure to disease. Gender and inter-generational issues among Indigenous Peoples also are complex. As social groups with identities that are often distinct from dominant groups in their national societies, Indigenous Peoples are frequently among the most marginalised and vulnerable segments of the population. As a result, their economic, social, and legal status often limits their capacity to defend their interests in and rights to lands, territories, and other productive resources, and/or restricts their ability to participate in and benefit from development. At the same time, the Bank recognises that Indigenous Peoples play a vital role in sustainable development and that their rights are increasingly being addressed under both domestic and international law.

3. *Identification.* Because of the varied and changing contexts in which Indigenous Peoples live and because there is no universally accepted definition of "Indigenous Peoples," this policy does not define the term. Indigenous Peoples may be referred to in different countries by such terms as 'indigenous ethnic minorities,' 'aboriginals,' 'hill tribes,' 'minority nationalities,' 'scheduled tribes,' or 'tribal groups.'

4. For purposes of this policy, the term 'Indigenous Peoples' is used in a generic sense to refer to a distinct, vulnerable, social and cultural group[6] possessing the following characteristics in varying degrees:

   (a) self-identification as members of a distinct indigenous cultural group and recognition of this identity by others;

   (b) collective attachment to geographically distinct habitats or ancestral territories in the project area and to the natural resources in these habitats and territories;[7]

   (c) customary cultural, economic, social, or political institutions that are separate from those of the dominant society and culture; and

(d) an indigenous language, often different from the official language of the country or region.

A group that has lost 'collective attachment to geographically distinct habitats or ancestral territories in the project area'; (paragraph 4 (b)) because of forced severance remains eligible for coverage under this policy.[8] Ascertaining whether a particular group is considered as 'Indigenous Peoples' for the purpose of this policy may require a technical judgment (see paragraph 8).

5. *Use of Country Systems.* The Bank may decide to use a country's systems to address environmental and social safeguard issues in a Bank-financed project that affects Indigenous Peoples. This decision is made in accordance with the requirements of the applicable Bank policy on country systems.[9]

Project Preparation

6. A project proposed for Bank financing that affects Indigenous Peoples requires:

   (a) screening by the Bank to identify whether Indigenous Peoples are present in, or have collective attachment to, the project area (see paragraph 8);

   (b) a social assessment by the borrower (sec paragraph 9 and Annex A);

   (c) a process of free, prior, and informed consultation with the affected Indigenous Peoples' communities at each stage of the project, and particularly during project preparation, to fully identify their views and ascertain their broad community support for the project (see paragraphs 10 and 11);

   (d) the preparation of an Indigenous Peoples' Plan (see paragraph 12 and Annex B) or an Indigenous Peoples' Planning Framework (see paragraph 13 and Annex C); and

   (e) disclosure of the draft Indigenous Peoples Plan or draft Indigenous Peoples' Planning Framework (see paragraph 15).

7. The level of detail necessary to meet the requirements

specified in paragraph 6 (b), (c), and (d) is proportional to the complexity of the proposed project and commensurate with the nature and scale of the proposed project's potential effects on the Indigenous Peoples, whether adverse or positive.

Screening

8. Early in project preparation, the Bank undertakes a screening to determine whether Indigenous Peoples (see paragraph 4) are present in, or have collective attachment to, the project area.[10] In conducting this screening, the Bank seeks the technical judgment of qualified social scientists with expertise on the social and cultural groups in the project area. The Bank also consults the Indigenous Peoples concerned and the borrower. The Bank may follow the borrower's framework for identification of Indigenous Peoples during project screening, when that framework is consistent with this policy.

Social Assessment

9. *Analysis.* If, based on the screening, the Bank concludes that Indigenous Peoples are present in, or have collective attachment to, the project area, the borrower undertakes a social assessment to evaluate the project's potential positive and adverse effects on the Indigenous Peoples, and to examine project alternatives where adverse effects may be significant. The breadth, depth, and type of analysis in the social assessment are proportional to the nature and scale of the proposed project's potential effects on the Indigenous Peoples, whether such effects are positive or adverse (see Annex A for details). To carry out the social assessment, the borrower engages social scientists whose qualifications, experience, and terms of reference are acceptable to the Bank.

10. *Consultation and Participation.* Where the project affects Indigenous Peoples, the borrower engages in free, prior, and informed consultation with them. To ensure such consultation, the borrower:

    (a) establishes an appropriate gender and intergenerationally inclusive framework that provides opportunities for consultation at each stage of project preparation and implementation among the borrower, the affected Indigenous Peoples' communities, the Indigenous Peoples Organisations (IPOs) if any, and other local Civil Society Organisations (CSOs) identified by the affected Indigenous Peoples' communities;

(b) uses consultation methods[11] appropriate to the social and cultural values of the affected Indigenous Peoples' communities and their local conditions and, in designing these methods, gives special attention to the concerns of Indigenous women, youth, and children and their access to development opportunities and benefits; and

(c) provides the affected Indigenous Peoples' communities with all relevant information about the project (including an assessment of potential adverse effects of the project on the affected Indigenous Peoples' communities) in a culturally appropriate manner at each stage of project preparation and implementation.

11. In deciding whether to proceed with the project, the borrower ascertains, on the basis of the social assessment (see paragraph 9) and the free, prior, and informed consultation (see paragraph 10), whether the affected Indigenous Peoples' communities provide their broad support to the project. Where there is such support, the borrower prepares a detailed report that documents:

(a) the findings of the social assessment;

(b) the process of free, prior, and informed consultation with the affected Indigenous Peoples' communities;

(c) additional measures, including project design modification, that may be required to address adverse effects on the Indigenous Peoples and to provide them with culturally appropriate project benefits;

(d) recommendations for free, prior, and informed consultation with and participation by Indigenous Peoples' communities during project implementation, monitoring, and evaluation; and

(e) any formal agreements reached with Indigenous Peoples' communities and/or the IPOs.

The Bank reviews the process and the outcome of the consultation carried out by the borrower to satisfy itself that the affected Indigenous Peoples' communities have provided their broad support to the project. The Bank pays particular attention to the social assessment and to the record and outcome of the free, prior, and informed consultation with the affected Indigenous Peoples' communities as a basis for ascertaining whether there is such support. The Bank does not proceed further with project processing if it is unable to ascertain that such support exists.

Indigenous Peoples Plan / Planning Framework

12. *Indigenous Peoples Plan.* On the basis of the social assessment and in consultation with the affected Indigenous Peoples' communities, the borrower prepares an Indigenous Peoples Plan (IPP) that sets out the measures through which the borrower will ensure that (a) Indigenous Peoples affected by the project receive culturally appropriate social and economic benefits, and (b) when potential adverse effects on Indigenous Peoples are identified, those adverse effects are avoided, minimised, mitigated, or compensated for (see Annex B for details). The IPP is prepared in a flexible and pragmatic manner,[12] and its level of detail varies depending on the specific project and the nature of effects to be addressed. The borrower integrates the IPP into the project design. When Indigenous Peoples are the sole or the overwhelming majority of direct project beneficiaries, the elements of an IPP should be included in the overall project design, and a separate IPP is not required. In such cases, the Project Appraisal Document (PAD) includes a brief summary of how the project complies with the policy, in particular, the IPP requirements.

13. *Indigenous Peoples' Planning Framework.* Some projects involve the preparation and implementation of annual investment programs or multiple subprojects.[13] In such cases, and when the Bank's screening indicates that Indigenous Peoples are likely to be present in, or have

collective attachment to, the project area, but their presence or collective attachment cannot be determined until the programs or sub-projects are identified, the borrower prepares an Indigenous Peoples Planning Framework (IPPF). IPPF provides for the screening and review of these programs or sub-projects in a manner consistent with this policy (see Annex C for details). The borrower integrates the IPPF into the project design.

14. *Preparation of Programme and Subproject IPPs.* If the screening of an individual programme or sub-project identified in the IPPF indicates that Indigenous Peoples are present in, or have collective attachment to, the area of the programme or sub-project, the borrower ensures that, before the individual program or subproject is implemented, a social assessment is carried out and an IPP is prepared in accordance with the requirements of this policy. The borrower provides each IPP to the Bank for review before the respective programme or sub-project is considered eligible for Bank financing.[14]

Disclosure

15. The borrower makes the social assessment report and draft IPP/IPPF available to the affected Indigenous Peoples' communities in an appropriate form, manner, and language.[15] Before project appraisal, the borrower sends the social assessment and draft IPP/IPPF to the Bank for review.[16] Once the Bank accepts the documents as providing an adequate basis for project appraisal, the Bank makes them available to the public in accordance with The World Bank Policy on Disclosure of Information, and the borrower makes them available to the affected Indigenous Peoples' communities in the same manner as the earlier draft documents.

Special Considerations

Lands and Related Natural Resources

16. Indigenous Peoples are closely tied to land, forests, water, wildlife, and other natural resources, and therefore special considerations apply if the project affects such ties. In this situation, when carrying out the social assessment

and preparing the IPP/IPPF, the borrower pays particular attention to:

(a) the customary rights[17] of the Indigenous Peoples, both individual and collective, pertaining to lands or territories that they traditionally owned, or customarily used or occupied, and where access to natural resources is vital to the sustainability of their cultures and livelihoods;

(b) the need to protect such lands and resources against illegal intrusion or encroachment;

(c) the cultural and spiritual values that the Indigenous Peoples attribute to such lands and resources; and

(d) Indigenous Peoples' natural resources management practices and the long-term sustainability of such practices.

17. If the project involves (a) activities that are contingent on establishing legally recognised rights to lands and territories that Indigenous Peoples have traditionally owned or customarily used or occupied (such as land titling projects), or (b) the acquisition of such lands, the IPP sets forth an action plan for the legal recognition of such ownership, occupation, or usage. Normally, the action plan is carried out before project implementation; in some cases, however, the action plan may need to be carried out concurrently with the project itself. Such legal recognition may take the following forms:

(a) full legal recognition of existing customary land tenure systems of Indigenous Peoples; or

(b) conversion of customary usage rights to communal and/or individual ownership rights.

If neither option is possible under domestic law, the IPP includes measures for legal recognition of perpetual or long-term renewable custodial or use rights.

Commercial Development of Natural and Cultural Resources

18. If the project involves the commercial development of natural resources (such as minerals, hydrocarbon resources, forests, water, or hunting/fishing grounds) on

lands or territories that Indigenous Peoples traditionally owned, or customarily used or occupied, the borrower ensures that as part of the free, prior, and informed consultation process the affected communities are informed of (a) their rights to such resources under statutory and customary law, (b) the scope and nature of the proposed commercial development and the parties interested or involved in such development, and (c) the potential effects of such development on the Indigenous Peoples' livelihoods, environments, and use of such resources. The borrower includes in the IPP arrangements to enable the Indigenous Peoples to share equitably in the benefits[18] to be derived from such commercial development; at a minimum, the IPP arrangements must ensure that the Indigenous Peoples receive, in a culturally appropriate manner, benefits, compensation, and rights to due process at least equivalent to that to which any landowner with full legal title to the land would be entitled in the case of commercial development on their land.

19. If the project involves the commercial development of Indigenous Peoples' cultural resources and knowledge (for example, pharmacological or artistic), the borrower ensures that as part of the free, prior, and informed consultation process, the affected communities are informed of (a) their rights to such resources under statutory and customary law; (b) the scope and nature of the proposed commercial development and the parties interested or involved in such development; and (c) the potential effects of such development on Indigenous Peoples' livelihoods, environments, and use of such resources. Commercial development of the cultural resources and knowledge of these Indigenous Peoples is conditional upon their prior agreement to such development. The IPP reflects the nature and content of such agreements and includes arrangements to enable Indigenous Peoples to receive benefits in a culturally appropriate way and share equitably in the benefits to be derived from such commercial development.

Physical Relocation of Indigenous Peoples

20. Because physical relocation of Indigenous Peoples is particularly complex and may have significant adverse impacts on their identity, culture, and customary livelihoods, the Bank requires the borrower to explore alternative projected signs to avoid physical relocation of Indigenous Peoples. In exceptional circumstances, when it is not feasible to avoid relocation, the borrower will not carry out such relocation without obtaining broad support for it from the affected Indigenous Peoples' communities as part of the free, prior, and informed consultation process. In such cases, the borrower prepares are settlement plan in accordance with the requirements of OP4.12, *Involuntary Resettlement*, that is compatible with the Indigenous Peoples' cultural preferences, and includes a land-based resettlement strategy. As part of the resettlement plan, the borrower documents the results of the consultation process. Where possible, the resettlement plan should allow the affected Indigenous Peoples to return to the lands and territories they traditionally owned, or customarily used or occupied, if the reasons for their relocation cease to exist.

21. In many countries, the lands set aside as legally designated parks and protected areas may overlap with lands and territories that Indigenous Peoples traditionally owned, or customarily used or occupied. The Bank recognises the significance of these rights of ownership, occupation, or usage, as well as the need for long-term sustainable management of critical ecosystems. Therefore, involuntary restrictions on Indigenous Peoples' access to legally designated parks and protected areas, in particular access to their sacred sites, should be avoided. In exceptional circumstances, where it is not feasible to avoid restricting access, the borrower prepares, with the free, prior, and informed consultation of the affected Indigenous Peoples' communities, a process framework in accordance with the provisions of OP 4.12. The process framework provides guidelines for preparation, during project implementation, of an individual parks and protected areas' management plan, and ensures that the

Indigenous Peoples participate in the design, implementation, monitoring, and evaluation of the management plan, and share equitably in the benefits of the parks and protected areas. The management plan should give priority to collaborative arrangements that enable the Indigenous, as the custodians of the resources, to continue to use them in an ecologically sustainable manner.

Indigenous Peoples and Development

22. In furtherance of the objectives of this policy, the Bank may, at a member country's request, support the country in its development planning and poverty reduction strategies by providing financial assistance for a variety of initiatives designed to:

 (a) strengthen local legislation, as needed, to establish legal recognition of the customary or traditional land tenure systems of Indigenous Peoples;

 (b) make the development process more inclusive of Indigenous Peoples by incorporating their perspectives in the design of development programs and poverty reduction strategies, and providing them with opportunities to benefit more fully from development programs through policy and legal reforms, capacity building, and free, prior, and informed consultation and participation;

 (c) support the development priorities of Indigenous Peoples through programs (such as community-driven development programs and locally managed social funds) developed by governments in cooperation with Indigenous Peoples;

 (d) address the gender[19] and intergenerational issues that exist among many Indigenous Peoples, including the special needs of indigenous women, youth, and children;

 (e) prepare participatory profiles of Indigenous Peoples to document their culture, demographic structure, gender and inter-generational relations and social organisation, institutions, production systems, religious beliefs, and resource use patterns;

(f) strengthen the capacity of Indigenous Peoples' communities and IPOs to prepare, implement, monitor, and evaluate development programs;

(g) strengthen the capacity of government agencies responsible for providing development services to Indigenous Peoples;

(h) protect indigenous knowledge, including by strengthening intellectual property rights; and

(i) facilitate partnerships among the government, IPOs, CSOs, and the private sector to promote Indigenous Peoples' development programs.

OP 4.10, Annex A - Social Assessment

These policies were prepared for use by World Bank staff and are not necessarily a complete treatment of the subject.

OP 4.10 – Annex A July, 2005

1. The breadth, depth, and type of analysis required for the social assessment are proportional to the nature and scale of the proposed project's potential effects on the Indigenous Peoples.
2. The social assessment includes the following elements as needed:
   (a) A review, on a scale appropriate to the project, of the legal and institutional framework applicable to Indigenous Peoples.

   (b) Gathering of baseline information on the demographic, social, cultural, and political characteristics of the affected Indigenous Peoples' communities, the land and territories that they have traditionally owned or customarily used or occupied, and the natural resources on which they depend.

   (c) Taking the review and baseline information into account, the identification of key project stakeholders and the elaboration of a culturally appropriate process for consulting with the Indigenous Peoples at each stage of project preparation and implementation (see paragraph 9 of this policy).

(d) An assessment, based on free, prior, and informed consultation, with the affected Indigenous Peoples' communities, of the potential adverse and positive effects of the project. Critical to the determination of potential adverse impacts is an analysis of the relative vulnerability of, and risks to, the affected Indigenous Peoples' communities given their distinct circumstances and close ties to land and natural resources, as well as their lack of access to opportunities relative to other social groups in the communities, regions, or national societies in which they live.

(e) The identification and evaluation, based on free, prior, and informed consultation with the affected Indigenous Peoples' communities, of measures necessary to avoid adverse effects, or if such measures are not feasible, the identification of measures to minimise, mitigate, or compensate for such effects, and to ensure that the Indigenous Peoples receive culturally appropriate benefits under the project.

OP 4.10, Annex B - Indigenous Peoples' Plan

These policies were prepared for use by World Bank staff and are not necessarily a complete treatment of the subject.

OP 4.10 – Annex B July, 2005

1. The Indigenous Peoples Plan (IPP) is prepared in a flexible and pragmatic manner, and its level of detail varies depending on the specific project and the nature of effects to be addressed.
2. The IPP includes the following elements, as needed:

   (a) A summary of the information referred to in Annex A, paragraph 2 (a) and (b).

   (b) A summary of the social assessment.

   (c) A summary of results of the free, prior, and informed consultation with the affected Indigenous Peoples' communities that was carried out during project preparation (Annex A) and that led to broad community support for the project.

(d) A framework for ensuring free, prior, and informed consultation with the affected Indigenous Peoples' communities during project implementation (see paragraph 10 of this policy).

(e) An action plan of measures to ensure that the Indigenous Peoples receive social and economic benefits that are culturally appropriate, including, if necessary, measures to enhance the capacity of the project implementing agencies.

(f) When potential adverse effects on Indigenous Peoples are identified, an appropriate action plan of measures to avoid, minimise, mitigate, or compensate for these adverse effects.

(g) The cost estimates and financing plan for the IPP.

(h) Accessible procedures appropriate to the project to address grievances by the affected Indigenous Peoples' communities arising from project implementation. When designing the grievance procedures, the borrower takes into account the availability of judicial recourse and customary dispute settlement mechanisms among the Indigenous Peoples.

(i) Mechanisms and benchmarks appropriate to the project for monitoring, evaluating, and reporting on the implementation of the IPP. The monitoring and evaluation mechanisms should include arrangements for the free, prior, and informed consultation with the affected Indigenous Peoples' communities.

OP 4.10, Annex C - Indigenous Peoples' Planning Framework

These policies were prepared for use by World Bank staff and are not necessarily a complete treatment of the subject.

OP 4.10 – Annex C July, 2005

1. The Indigenous Peoples Planning Framework (IPPF) sets out:

   (a) The types of programs and sub-projects likely to be proposed for financing under the project.

(b) The potential positive and adverse effects of such programs or subprojects on Indigenous Peoples.

(c) A plan for carrying out the social assessment (see Annex A) for such programs or sub-projects.

(d) A framework for ensuring free, prior, and informed consultation with the affected Indigenous Peoples' communities at each stage of project preparation and implementation (see paragraph 10 of this policy).

(e) Institutional arrangements (including capacity building where necessary) for screening project-supported activities, evaluating their effects on the Indigenous Peoples, preparing IPPs, and addressing any grievances.

(f) Monitoring and reporting arrangements, including mechanisms and benchmarks appropriate to the project.

(g) Disclosure arrangements for IPPs to be prepared under the IPPF.

Notes

1. This policy should be read together with other relevant Bank policies, including *Environmental Assessment* (OP 4.01), *Natural Habitats* (OP 4.04), *Pest Management* (OP4.09), *Physical Cultural Resources* (OP/BP4.11), *Involuntary Resettlement* (OP 4.12), *Forests* (OP4.36), and *Safety of Dams* (OP4.37).

2.. 'Bank' includes IBRD and IDA; 'loans' includes IBRD loans, IDA credits, IDA grants, IBRD and IDA guarantees, and Project Preparation Facility (PPF) advances, but does not include development policy loans, credits, or grants. For social aspects of development policy operations, see OP 8.60, *Development Policy Lending*, paragraph 10. The term "borrower" includes, wherever the context requires, the recipient of an IDA grant, the guarantor of an IBRD loan, and the project implementing agency, if it is different from the borrower.

3. This policy applies to all components of the project that affect Indigenous Peoples, regardless of the source of financing.

4. 'Free, prior, and informed consultation with the affected Indigenous Peoples' communities' refers to a culturally appropriate and collective decision making process subsequent to meaningful and good faith consultation and informed

participation regarding the preparation and implementation of the project. It does not constitute a veto right for individuals or groups (see paragraph 10).

5. For details on 'broad community support to the project by the affected Indigenous Peoples,' see paragraph 11.
6. The policy does not set an *a priori* minimum numerical threshold since groups of Indigenous Peoples may be very small in number and their size may make them more vulnerable.
7. 'Collective attachment' means that for generations there has been a physical presence in and economic ties to lands and territories traditionally owned, or customarily used or occupied, by the group concerned, including areas that hold special significance for it, such as sacred sites. 'Collective attachment' also refers to the attachment of transhumant/nomadic groups to the territory they use on a seasonal or cyclical basis.
8. 'Forced severance' refers to loss of collective attachment to geographically distinct habitats or ancestral territories occurring within the concerned group members' lifetime because of conflict, government resettlement programs, dispossession from their lands, natural calamities, or incorporation of such territories into an urban area. For purposes of this policy, 'urban area' normally means a city or a large town, and takes into account all of the following characteristics, no single one of which is definitive: (a) the legal designation of the area as urban under domestic law, (b) high population density, and (c) high proportion of nonagricultural economic activities relative to agricultural activities.
9. The currently applicable Bank policy is OP/BP 4.00, *Piloting the Use of Borrower Systems to Address Environmental and Social Safeguard Issues in Bank-Supported Projects*. Applicable only to pilot projects using borrower systems, the policy includes requirements that such systems be designed to meet the policy objectives and adhere to the operational principles related to Indigenous Peoples identified in OP 4.00 (see Table A1).
10. The screening may be carried out independently or as part of a project environmental assessment (see OP 4.01, *Environmental Assessment,* paragraphs 3, 8).
11. Such consultation methods (including using indigenous languages, allowing time for consensus building, and selecting appropriate venues) facilitate the articulation by Indigenous Peoples of their views and preferences. The *Indigenous Peoples Guidebook* (forthcoming) will provide good practice guidance on this and other matters.

12. When non-Indigenous Peoples live in the same area with Indigenous Peoples, the IPP should attempt to avoid creating unnecessary inequities for other poor and marginal social groups.
13. Such projects include community-driven development projects, social funds, sector investment operations, and financial intermediary loans.
14. If the Bank considers the IPPF to be adequate for the purpose, however, the Bank may agree with the borrower that prior Bank review of the IPP is not needed. In such case, the Bank reviews the IPP and its implementation as part of supervision (see OP 13.05 *Project Supervision*)
15. The social assessment and IPP require wide dissemination among the affected Indigenous Peoples' communities using culturally appropriate methods and locations. In the case of an IPPF, the document is disseminated using IPOs at the appropriate national, regional, or local levels to reach Indigenous Peoples who are likely to be affected by the project. Where IPOs do not exist, the document may be disseminated using other CSOs as appropriate.
16. An exception to the requirement that the IPP (or IPPF) be prepared as a condition of appraisal may be made with the approval of Bank management for projects meeting the requirements of OP 8.00, *Rapid Response to Crises and Emergencies.* In such cases, management's approval stipulates a timetable and budget for preparation of the social assessment and IPP or of the IPPF.
17. 'Customary rights' to lands and resources refers to patterns of long-standing community land and resource usage in accordance with Indigenous Peoples' customary laws, values, customs, and traditions, including seasonal or cyclical use, rather than formal legal title to land and resources issued by the State.
18. The *Indigenous Peoples Guidebook* (forthcoming) will provide good practice guidance on this matter.
19. See OP/BP 4.20, *Gender and Development.*

17

Asian Development Bank (ADB) Policy on Indigenous Peoples

The Bank's Policy on Indigenous Peoples, April 1998

Abbreviations

COSS	Country Operational Strategy Study
DMC	Developing Member Country
IDB	Inter-American Development Bank
ILO	International Labour Organisation
ISA	Initial Social Assessment
OESD	Office of Environment and Social Development
PPTA	Project Preparatory Technical Assistance
RRP	Report and Recommendation of the President
UNICED	United Nation Conference on Environment Programme
UNDP	United Nations Development Programme

(I) Introduction

1. Indigenous peoples[1] can be regarded as one of the largest vulnerable segments of society. While differing significantly in terms of culture, identity, economic systems, and social institutions, indigenous peoples as a whole most often reflect specific disadvantage in terms of social indicators, economic status, and quality of life.

Indigenous peoples often are not able to participate equally in development processes and share in the benefits of development, and often are not adequately represented in national social, economic, and political processes that direct development. While constituting a relatively small part of the population of the Bank's region, indigenous peoples and their potential vulnerability must be regarded as significant in the Bank's development efforts and interventions.

2. It is neither desirable nor possible to insulate or exclude indigenous peoples from development. Like dominant or mainstream populations, the group or groups in a country that are politically, economically, and culturally most powerful indigenous peoples have developmental aspirations. However, indigenous peoples may not benefit from development programs designed to meet the needs and aspirations of dominant or mainstream populations, and may not be given the opportunity to participate in the planning of such development. There is increasing concern in the international development community that indigenous peoples be afforded opportunities to participate in and benefit from development equally with other segments of society, and have a role and be able to participate in the design of development interventions that affect them.

3. The legislation and policies of most member countries of the Bank recognise indigenous peoples as citizens. In practice, however, indigenous peoples often experience disadvantage in interaction with dominant and mainstream populations especially as relates to development. Beyond not benefiting from development nor participating in the planning of development, indigenous peoples can be disadvantaged by of access to ancestral lands and the natural resources and other sources of income contained in these lands, loss of culture, social structures, and institutions, loss of indigenous knowledge, loss of recognition as indigenous peoples, and a lack of opportunities for effective participation in national political and economic processes. Lack of participation in development combined with the loss of

access to land and resources have in many cases marginalised indigenous peoples. In some extreme cases, indigenous peoples have suffered physical oppression. In a few cases, indigenous cultures have disintegrated or disappeared.

4. In its operations, the Bank must recognise and respect the sovereignty of its member countries, including national legislation and policy relating to indigenous peoples and at the same time, recognise a responsibility for ensuring equality of opportunity for indigenous peoples, and that its operations and assistance to developing member countries (DMCs) do not negatively affect the welfare and interests of indigenous peoples. If a Bank intervention does affect indigenous peoples negatively, adequate measures must be taken to mitigate the negative impact, or make certain that a compensation plan ensuring that project affected people are as well off with the project as without is prepared and implemented.

5. This paper addresses policy approaches toward recognising the circumstances of indigenous peoples and identifying measures toward satisfying their needs and aspirations. The paper focuses on the participation of indigenous peoples in development and mitigation of undesired effects of development. Section II provides a definition of indigenous peoples; Section III addresses issues of indigenous peoples in development; Section IV discusses laws and international conventions that apply and practices of comparator institutions; Section V presents a set of proposed policy objectives, and operational approaches and procedures, and Section VI addresses organisational implications and resource requirements of formal Bank policy addressing indigenous peoples. Section VII presents specific policy recommendations.

6. This paper is a policy document, setting out policy proposals relating to indigenous peoples in Bank operations. This policy initiative is undertaken in parallel with specific development interventions of the Bank that would address the needs and concerns of indigenous peoples' projects designed to provide specific developmental support to indigenous peoples.

(II) Definition of Indigenous Peoples

7. Developing a single, specific definition or identification for indigenous peoples would be difficult. Within the Asian and Pacific Region, individual indigenous people's communities reflect tremendous diversity in their cultures, histories and current circumstances. Country by country, the relationships between indigenous peoples and dominant or mainstream groups of society vary.

8. From the perspective of developing a working definition of indigenous peoples for use in Bank operations, several aspects must be considered. A starting point would be to define indigenous peoples on the basis of characteristics they display. Two significant characteristics would be (i) descent from population groups present in a given area, most often before modem states or territories were created and before modem borders were defined, and (ii) maintenance of cultural and social identities, and social, economic, cultural, and political institutions separate from mainstream or dominant societies and cultures. In some cases, over recent centuries, tribal groups or cultural minorities have migrated into areas to which they are not indigenous, but have established a presence and continue to maintain a definite and separate social and cultural identity and related social institutions. In such cases, the second identifying characteristic would carry greater weight.

9. Additional characteristics often ascribed to indigenous peoples include (i) selfidentification and identification by others as being part of a distinct indigenous cultural group, and the display of desire to preserve that cultural identity, (ii) a linguistic identity different from that of the dominant society, (iii) social, cultural, economic, and political traditions and institutions distinct from the dominant culture, (iv) economic systems oriented more toward traditional systems of production than mainstream systems, and (v) unique ties and attachments to traditional habitats and ancestral territories and natural resources in these habitats and territories.

10. Indigenous peoples also are described with reference to

their ways of life. In many cases, indigenous peoples live in separated communities or cultural or ethnic groupings. Such communities and groupings often are located in areas geographically distant from urban centers and often function at the periphery of the political, social, cultural, and economic systems of the dominant or mainstream society. At the same time, however, it is not unusual to find indigenous peoples communities on the fringes of urban areas, comprising indigenous peoples' who have migrated but remain distinct from the mainstream. Indigenous people's communities in a given country can reflect varying degrees of acculturation and integration into the dominant or mainstream society.

11. In specific development interventions supported by the Bank, the national legislation of the country in which the development intervention is taking place provides a basis for defining indigenous peoples. This includes constitutional, statutory, and customary law, as well as international law, including any international conventions to which the country is a party. It would be necessary that other country-specific considerations be taken into account.

12. As a working definition to be employed in the Bank's operations as they affect indigenous peoples, indigenous peoples should be regarded as those with a social or cultural identity distinct from the dominant or mainstream society, which makes them vulnerable to being disadvantaged in the processes of development. Determination of a distinct identity for indigenous peoples would be based in the requirements of applicable national law and the applicability of characteristics described in paras. 8-11 above. The application of any definition of indigenous peoples should work to differentiate between indigenous peoples and other cultural and ethnic minorities for which indigenous status is not an issue; the broader protection of vulnerable groups is an issue addressed in other policies and practices of the Bank.

13. Case-specific identification of indigenous peoples affected by Bank operations and approaches to addressing specific indigenous peoples' concerns would be addressed in the

process of initial social assessment and the preparation of an indigenous peoples plan (see paras. 34-40 and the Appendix).

(III) Indigenous Peoples and Development

(A) Indigenous Peoples and Development

14. As socioeconomic development takes place, many development initiatives are extending farther into geographically remote areas often considered the traditional homelands of indigenous peoples; these areas offer resources such as forests, minerals, and hydropower potential. Roads, power transmission lines, and other infrastructure development initiatives similarly are extending into the traditional areas of indigenous peoples. In parallel with physical and economic development, dominant and mainstream populations and cultures also are extending into the traditional areas of indigenous peoples.

15. Protection of indigenous peoples from development or maintenance of a status quo for indigenous peoples should not be a development objective. At the same time, it is not uncommon that interests of indigenous peoples differ from those of the mainstream, and that development policies and approaches addressing the interests of dominant and mainstream communities conflict with the interests of indigenous peoples. What may be in the broad national interest may not be in the specific interests of indigenous peoples, and development emerging from dominant and mainstream community-oriented initiatives may arrive in forms not consistent with indigenous peoples' interests or concerns.

16. Development as it most often is pursued is intended to meet national goals and the interests of dominant and mainstream societies. Reducing poverty and improving the quality of life of people in general most often are the primary objectives of development. However, it is not always the case that poverty reduction and improvement in the quality of life realised from development extend equally to all segments of society, or that improvement reaches each segment of society. Moreover, in

mainstream-oriented economic development policies, indigenous people's communities may bear a disproportionate burden of the negative social, economic, and environmental effects that such development projects may bring, without realising commensurate benefits.

(B) Goals and Objectives of Development

17. There may be differences in views between dominant and mainstream societies and indigenous people's communities as to the broad goals and objectives that development should pursue. Development viewed from the mainstream often is measured in terms of economic advancement or gain and improvement in quality of life, and most often places emphasis on economic growth. From the development perspective of indigenous peoples, in addition to economic advancement, there may also be concern for social, cultural, environmental, and community aspects of development as a combination of economic advancement and social, cultural, and community development. Indigenous peoples sometimes view the principles and efforts of mainstream development as inappropriate or unsustainable, and as an intrusion into traditional ways of life. The physical intrusions of development interventions into the traditional domains of indigenous peoples, and social intrusions into indigenous cultures, can be viewed by indigenous peoples and others as a violation of human rights, rights to land, and rights associated with the maintenance of culture.

(C) Culture and Development

18. Indigenous peoples' desires to protect their cultural identities and to preserve aspects of culture based in ancestral lands and resources is receiving increasing recognition within the international development community. Increasing recognition is being given to the principle of indigenous peoples determining their own pace and path of development, and there is increasing recognition that social and cultural diversity is in the interest of society and is not an obstacle to national development or economic stability. There is increasing recognition that there is dignity in all cultures, that

there should be equality in opportunity for all segments of society, and that all segments of society deserve opportunities for equal access to both the factors and the benefits of development.

(IV) Laws and Conventions Affecting Indigenous Peoples

(A) National Laws and Practices

19. With a substantial portion of the world's indigenous peoples living in Asia and the Pacific, virtually every country in the region has an indigenous population. While the effectiveness of provisions may vary, some countries recognise the unique status of indigenous peoples and offer the privileges and protections of citizenship. Few countries have enacted laws that recognise any rights of indigenous peoples to ancestral lands, or that support indigenous peoples regaining and strengthening their social, cultural, and legal institutions. In many cases, enforcement of laws that may exist has been inadequate.
20. Some countries have experienced conflicts between interests of indigenous peoples and interests of dominant and mainstream communities. These conflicts most often relate to control over and exploitation of natural resources in the areas indigenous peoples claim as traditional domains. Appropriation of ancestral territories or resources in these territories by governments or external interests most often is justified as a part of economic development and growth. Indigenous peoples' sparse occupation of large areas of land and nonintensive use of resources often is characterised by external interests as economic inefficiency or lost opportunity. Indigenous peoples' land and resource management practices sometimes are viewed as unsustainable or environmentally damaging.
21. At the national level, in some cases, new laws, policies, and other measures may be necessary to reconcile competing demands and conflicting interests, especially if interests of indigenous peoples are to be protected. In any case, however, the Bank must respect the will of governments, including legislation and policy that exists

and the power of eminent domain that governments possess. Country programs and project selection will be developed in cooperation with governments. When difficulties are encountered, the Bank may be able to provide guidance or assistance through mechanisms such as policy dialogue and technical assistance.

(B) International Conventions and Declarations

22. The international community has shown increasing concern for the protection of the rights of indigenous peoples. Conventions and declarations of the international community provide a broad framework, as well as specific statements regarding the protection of indigenous peoples and their interests, cultures, ways of life, cultural survival, and development. It may be noted that some international instruments relating to indigenous peoples have not been ratified by large numbers of the international community.

23. The United Nations *Universal Declaration of Human Rights* (1948) and *International Covenant on Civil and Political Rights* (1966) have specific significance for indigenous peoples. The *Universal Declaration* provides a common standard for the human rights of all peoples and all nations, and proclaims the importance of traditional, political, and civil rights, as well as basic economic social and cultural rights. The *Covenant* spells out civil and political rights and guiding principles based on the Universal Declaration.

24. The 1957 International Labour Organisation (ILO) Convention No. 107, *Protection and Integration of Indigenous and Other Tribal and Semi-Tribal Populations in Independent Countries,* addresses the right of indigenous peoples to pursue material well-being and spiritual development, and was the first international instrument in specific support of indigenous peoples. Largely because of its view that indigenous peoples should be integrated into the larger society, a view that subsequently came to be seen by many as inappropriate, Convention No. 107 was followed in 1989 by ILO Convention 169, *Convention Concerning Indigenous and Tribal Peoples in Independent Countries.*

25. Convention No. 169 presents the fundamental concept that the way of life of indigenous and tribal peoples should and will survive, as well as the view indigenous and tribal peoples and their traditional organisations should be closely involved in the planning and implementation of development projects that affect them. As the most comprehensive and most current international legal instrument to address issues vital to indigenous and tribal peoples, Convention No. 169 includes articles that deal with consultation and participation, social security and health, human development, and the environment. To date, Convention No. 169 has been ratified by only a few countries, and so far by none in the Asian and Pacific Region.

26. *Agenda 21* adopted by the United Nations Conference on Environment and Development (UNCED) in 1992 recognises the actual and potential contribution of indigenous and tribal peoples to sustainable development. The 1992 *Convention on Biodiversity* calls on contracting parties to respect traditional indigenous knowledge with regard to biodiversity and its sustainable use. The *Vienna Declaration and Programme of Action* emerging from the 1993 World Conference on Human Rights recognises the dignity and unique cultural contributions of indigenous peoples, and strongly reaffirms the commitment of the international community to the economic, social, and cultural well-being of indigenous peoples and their enjoyment of the fruits of sustainable development.

27. The United Nation's 1993 *Draft Declaration on the Rights of Indigenous Peoples*, developed with the direct participation of indigenous peoples representatives and currently under consideration within the United Nations, addresses issues such as the right to participation, the right of indigenous peoples to direct their own development, the right of indigenous peoples to determine and develop priorities and strategies for the development or use of ancestral territories and resources, and the right to self-determination. The emerging concern for indigenous peoples prompted the United Nations to declare 1993 as the International Year of the World's

Indigenous Peoples and the decade from December 1994 as the Indigenous Peoples' Decade.

(C) Practices of Other International Institutions

28. Among comparator organisations, World Bank policies and practices are the most relevant to the Bank. The World Bank's *Operational Directive 4.20: Indigenous Peoples* establishes specific approaches to indigenous peoples in World Bank operations. Through its operational directive, the World Bank recognises and takes into consideration issues such as the identification of indigenous peoples, the attachment of indigenous peoples to land and resources, and the significance of distinct linguistic and cultural identities, and the primarily subsistence nature of indigenous peoples' production systems. World Bank policy calls for indigenous peoples' informed and willing participation in development, and respect for indigenous peoples' dignity, human rights, and cultural uniqueness. For development interventions that affect indigenous peoples directly and significantly, an indigenous peoples' development plan is required.

29. Another comparator organisation with direct relevance to the Bank is the Inter- American Development Bank (IDB). While IDB does not have a specific policy addressing indigenous peoples, it does address their concerns through its operational activities, an approach IDB considers more relevant to the circumstances of its region. Operational processes relating to involuntary resettlement, poverty reduction, rural development, and environmental and social impact assessment all include specific consideration of indigenous peoples' concerns. In the IDB region, the poorest segments of society often are indigenous peoples, and projects are designed specifically to assist these groups. In the IDB, creation of special funds to support activities such as enterprise development and capacity building provide other avenues for the pursuit of issues relating to indigenous peoples. The representative offices that IDB maintains in its client countries provide a basis for country-specific consideration of indigenous peoples concerns.

30. Among United Nations agencies, the United Nations Development Programme (UNDP) has undertaken a number of programs to address indigenous peoples' concerns. In the Bank's region, the objectives of UNDP's Highland Peoples Programme, covering Cambodia, Lao People's Democratic Republic, Thailand, and Vietnam, are to increase organisational capacities and opportunities among highland communities, in participatory planning, management, and coordination; establish and/or reinforce exchange mechanisms and procedures; and work for the overall development of highland communities in the four countries covered.

(V) Policy Objectives, Processes and Approaches within the Bank

(A) Policy Objectives

31. In its operations, it is necessary that the Bank develop a policy and associated strategies and approaches that recognise the potential vulnerability of indigenous peoples in development processes, as well as ensure that indigenous peoples have opportunities to participate in and benefit equally from development. The Bank's strategies and approaches should avoid negatively affecting indigenous peoples, and provide adequate and appropriate compensation when a negative impact is unavoidable. The Bank's development efforts should ensure that development initiatives affecting indigenous peoples are effective and sustainable. Initiatives should be compatible in substance and structure with the affected peoples' culture and social and economic institutions, and commensurate with the needs, aspirations and demands of affected peoples. Initiatives should be conceived, planned, and implemented, to the maximum extent possible, with the informed consent of affected communities, and include respect for indigenous peoples' dignity, human rights, and cultural uniqueness.

32. Strategies and approaches to development that affect indigenous peoples must include clear mechanisms for accurate, objective analysis of their circumstances. Development processes must incorporate transparency

and accountability. A policy on indigenous peoples would apply to operations in both the public and the private sectors.

33. The strategies and approaches to be employed by the Bank should build on the existing strengths in its strategic framework and operational experience. A policy to address indigenous peoples would complement and support, and be complemented and supported by other Bank policies. Compliance with a policy on indigenous peoples would not obviate the requirement of compliance with other Bank policies.

(B) Operational Processes

1. Initial Social Assessment

34. As provided in Section 47 of the Bank's *Operations Manual*, an Initial Social Assessment (ISA) is required for every development project.[2] The ISA identifies intended project beneficiaries as well as groups that might be affected adversely. The ISA addresses people's needs, demands, and capacities, as well as the key social dimensions that a project must address; such as involuntary resettlement, poverty reduction, human development, gender and development, and vulnerable groups. As such, indigenous peoples would be a specific concern to be considered in the ISA process. The ISA should be undertaken as early as possible in the project development process, preferably by the time of the Project Preparatory Technical Assistance (PPTA) fact-finding or other preparatory studies, to ensure that all relevant social concerns will be addressed in project design.

35. If the ISA determines that indigenous peoples are likely to be affected significantly by a Bank intervention or that indigenous peoples are disadvantaged or vulnerable in an intervention because of their social or cultural identity, a specific indigenous peoples' plan addressing indigenous peoples and their concerns, that is time bound and that has appropriate budget provisions, must be developed (see paras. 37-40). This plan would be incorporated as an integral part of project design. A case-specific definition of "affected significantly" would be

guided by existing Bank practice relating to this matter.

36. While the ISA is a process that identifies populations that may be affected by a project and specific social dimensions that should be addressed, the indigenous peoples plan must focus specifically on indigenous peoples to be affected and specific socioeconomic issues that would be significant. The ISA would address definition and identification of indigenous peoples in the specific context of the project in question. Such definition and identification would consider all relevant factors, including country-specific considerations and national legislation and policy, as well as other factors (see paras. 7-13). Even in an intervention that does not require an indigenous peoples' plan, the circumstances and needs of an indigenous peoples' group if affected by an intervention generally would be considered in the ISA.

2. Indigenous Peoples Development Plan

37. For a Bank-assisted development project that affects indigenous peoples' adversely and significantly, an indigenous peoples plan acceptable to the Bank must be prepared. Beyond addressing indigenous peoples' populations and relevant social issues, the indigenous peoples plan must include specific measures and approaches to be taken to address issues affecting indigenous peoples. A project negatively affecting indigenous peoples must be appropriately redesigned to mitigate negative effects, or include an acceptable compensation plan; the provision of compensation should not be a substitute for efforts to avoid or mitigate negative effects a project may have. The indigenous peoples plan would form a basis for project implementation, and for monitoring and evaluation of how the project deals with indigenous peoples' issues. Specific components or provisions of the plan must be included in the project design; the plan should address questions of sustainability of the proposed project as well as questions of its implementation. The Appendix to this paper provides key elements to be considered in the creation of such a plan. Bank staff involved in the processing of a project affecting indigenous peoples must inform the government

or other project sponsors of the Bank's policy on indigenous peoples.

38. The responsibility for preparation of an indigenous peoples' plan acceptable to the Bank and for its implementation rests with the government or other project sponsors. The indigenous peoples' plan should be submitted to the Bank by the government or private sector project sponsor preferably along with the feasibility study for the project. The costs of an indigenous peoples' plan would affect and be part of the overall cost of a project, and implementation of the indigenous peoples plan would have effects on the overall implementation schedule of a project. The Bank would support the efforts of the government or other project sponsors, as necessary and appropriate, through (i) assistance in formulating and implementing the indigenous peoples' plan, (ii) assistance in formulating policies, strategies, laws, regulations and other specific actions related to indigenous peoples, (iii) providing technical assistance to strengthen the capacity of agencies responsible for indigenous peoples, and (iv) financing eligible costs of implementing the indigenous peoples' plan, if requested. For any project, the indigenous peoples' plan necessarily must be completed before project appraisal.

39. The indigenous peoples' plan would include an executive summary, with salient issues of this executive summary preferably to be included in the draft Report and Recommendation of the President (RRP) to be considered in the Management Review Meeting, and in every case in the final RRP for submission for Board of Directors' consideration.

40. Upon approval of a Bank policy on indigenous peoples, operational guidelines reflecting the above approaches and detailing specific steps to be taken will be prepared and issued. Until operational guidelines are prepared, existing staff instructions on indigenous peoples in Bank operations will apply.[3] In both the cases, OESD will continue to provide advice and assistance in matters related to indigenous peoples.

(C) Operational Approaches

41. In development efforts that affect indigenous peoples, it is necessary that the Bank integrate concern for indigenous peoples into each step of programming, project processing, and policy development cycles. Beyond program- and project-related considerations, it is likely that structural constraints could affect realisation of policy objectives. Such constraints may include a lack of (i) an appropriate legislative framework in DMCs, (ii) necessary capacity or relevant development institutions and agencies, (iii) detailed and objective knowledge and information about indigenous peoples and their circumstances, and (iv) accurate and effective representation of indigenous peoples. In addition to directly addressing the needs of indigenous peoples, strategies to overcome structural constraints should be explored. Effective approaches to information dissemination and communication with indigenous peoples communities should be identified, especially where conventional approaches to information dissemination and communication may not be effective. It may also be necessary to provide specific consideration to matters such as indigenous women's concerns.

42. Achievements that have been realised in the implementation of policies addressing indigenous peoples' concerns may form the basis for considering appropriate adjustments in borrowing countries' legislation and institutional channels. In this regard, it would be desirable that indigenous peoples' issues be addressed in project monitoring and evaluation activities, and that indigenous peoples' participate in monitoring and evaluation processes. Modalities for policy development could include policy dialogue and other appropriate technical assistance. Ideally, development of necessary strategies would be based on consultations involving the Bank, DMC governments, other project sponsors as appropriate, representatives of indigenous peoples, and other stakeholders.

43. Key issues that should be considered as the Bank addresses indigenous peoples matters, and the continuity

and development of indigenous peoples communities, include (i) legal recognition of ancestral domain and the traditional rights of indigenous peoples over land and resources, (ii) recognised legitimacy of the indigenous social and legal institutions of indigenous peoples, and (iii) recognition of the right of indigenous peoples to direct the course of their own development and change.

44. Institutional strengthening and capacity building support for indigenous peoples communities should be provided as necessary and appropriate. Similarly, as necessary and appropriate, institutional strengthening and capacity building support should be provided to relevant government entities when such support would increase the effectiveness and efficiency of such entities.

(VI) Organisational Implications and Resource Requirements

(A) Organisational Implications

45. The Office of Environment and Social Development (OESD) will hold primary organisational responsibility for implementation of the Bank's policy on indigenous peoples. OESD will provide guidance and assistance to other departments and offices on the application of the policy in Bank operations, and will consult with these departments and offices on the development of relevant operational practices and procedures.

46. OESD will be responsible for developing and coordinating operational guidelines for implementation and operationalisation of policy on indigenous peoples. These guidelines will be developed with the active input and cooperation of other departments and offices of the Bank. On an ongoing basis, OESD will continue to gather and disseminate relevant information to other units of the Bank. OESD will provide advice and guidance on indigenous peoples matters.

47. OESD will designate a Social Development Specialist as a Bank-wide focal point and resource person to provide specific advice and guidance on matters related to indigenous peoples in the Bank's operations. OESD will

hold responsibility for reporting as required on the implementation and application of an indigenous peoples policy.

48. The Programs Departments will be responsible for applying the policy on indigenous peoples as it relates to country programming, and for incorporating such policy aspects in the development of country strategies and in project and technical assistance identification. This process would be a part of policy dialogue with governments. As country level programming processes, including those related to the preparation of the Country Operational Strategy Study (COSS), are the initial steps in country-level project identification, concern for indigenous peoples matters would have significance in these processes. The Programs Departments would consider social development issues as they arise in country programming processes and in economic and sector work. Resident Missions would be country-level points of contact on matters relating to indigenous peoples and would provide advice to Headquarters staff. Headquarters would provide necessary support in this regard.

49. The Projects Departments will have responsibility for project-specific aspects of indigenous peoples policy, including making governments, project executing agencies, and other project sponsors aware of the Bank's policy provisions and requirements. This responsibility will apply to project identification, processing, implementation, and monitoring. The Projects Departments are normally responsible for the initial social assessment process, and for the development of appropriate indigenous peoples development plans when required.

50. The Office of Pacific Operations will hold responsibility for indigenous peoples' policy as it relates to operations in the Bank's Pacific DMCs.

51. The Post-Evaluation Office, through its post-evaluation function, will be responsible for assessing the effectiveness of the Bank's operations in implementing and applying

the policy on indigenous peoples, and the development of appropriate evaluation criteria.

(B) Resource Requirements

52. To address operational considerations related to indigenous peoples concerns as described in this paper, processing of projects that affect indigenous peoples may require longer processing times and additional resources for processing. Also required might be consultant and technical assistance resources. In addition to resources and time that would be required in preparing projects that affect indigenous peoples, projects that affect indigenous peoples may also involve efforts that address and work to alleviate structural constraints on the borrowing country and executing agency side. It would be necessary that adequate resources be made available.

53. With the adoption of a policy on indigenous peoples, the Bank will need to develop adequate internal institutional capacity to implement the policy effectively, and to make resources available to implement the provisions of the policy. It will be necessary to develop among staff, project and program staff especially, the capacity to recognise and deal effectively with issues and matters related to indigenous peoples. Initiatives in this regard should be explored. It would be necessary for OESD to have adequate resources to fulfill its coordinating and resources center role relating to indigenous peoples. Developing such capacity could be achieved through internal staff training efforts and other staff development activities. It would be desirable to recruit at least one staff with relevant operational experience and skills in matters related to indigenous peoples.

54. It would be necessary to provide support for institutional development and capacity building among indigenous peoples communities and within DMC governments. Such institutional development and capacity building support would be provided through project funding and through advisory and regional technical assistance.

55. In its loan and investment operations, resources necessary to satisfy existing staff instructions related to indigenous

peoples concerns already are being made available. In other aspects of indigenous peoples in Bank operations, such as the development of internal institutional capacity and capacity building, allocation of resources necessarily will be accommodated within current overall resource allocations. Prioritisation among current activities and possible new initiatives will be required.

56. In the Bank's current portfolio of projects, the number of projects directly affecting indigenous peoples is relatively small. However, with economic growth that extends the development horizon further from growth centers into more remote areas, as well as greater concern for indigenous peoples issues, it can be expected that the Bank will be involved in an increasing number of projects affecting indigenous peoples. It is expected that with a specific policy on indigenous peoples in place, project quality and the success of Bank interventions, as well as the effectiveness of the Bank's involvement in indigenous peoples matters, will be strengthened. Overall, it is expected that the increased benefits of development in general and the specific benefits of projects that affect indigenous peoples will outweigh the additional resource requirements placed on the Bank.

(VII) Policy on Indigenous Peoples

(A) A Policy on Indigenous Peoples in Bank Operations

57. A basic principle in the Bank's operations is examination of all implications and effects of the development initiatives and interventions it supports. The Bank operationalises this principle through the range of policies and practices, for example, relating to environment, involuntary resettlement, participation, social assessment, and gender and development. Consistent with this approach, it is recommended that the Bank establish policy and practices specifically addressing indigenous peoples affected by its operations, to reflect policy elements shown below.

(B) Policy Elements

58. For development interventions it supports or assists, the

Bank will ensure that affected populations and persons are at least as well-off as they would have been in the absence of the intervention, or that adequate and appropriate compensation be provided. Policy should ensure equality of opportunity for indigenous peoples. Policy must ensure that Bank interventions affecting indigenous peoples are (i) consistent with the needs and aspirations of affected indigenous peoples, (ii) compatible in substance and structure with affected indigenous peoples' culture and social and economic institutions, (iii) conceived, planned, and implemented with the informed participation of affected communities, (iv) equitable in terms of development efforts and impact, and (v) not imposing the negative effects of development on indigenous peoples without appropriate and acceptable compensation. A policy together with practices addressing indigenous peoples would be applied in parallel with and would not replace or supersede other existing Bank policies and practices. Each of the elements of policy and practice addressing indigenous peoples would be considered within the context of national development policies and approaches, and the fundamental relationship between the Bank and governments would be the basis for country-specific operations in a given country.

59. Policy on indigenous peoples will ensure that the process of initial social assessment mandated in Bank operations includes specific consideration of indigenous peoples as a potentially affected population. If the initial social assessment identifies indigenous peoples specifically as a significantly and adversely affected population, or vulnerable to being so affected, it will be ensured that an indigenous peoples' plan, as described in this working paper, is prepared by a government or other project sponsors.

60. The Bank will work to develop necessary and appropriate internal capacities for addressing indigenous peoples' matters in its operational activities.

61. The Bank will work with borrowing member countries as appropriate and necessary to support and assist the

development of capacities for addressing indigenous peoples matters. As necessary and appropriate, specific institutional development and capacity building support would be provided to both indigenous peoples communities and to governments, consistent with the Bank's policies and approaches addressing institutional development and capacity building.

62. In developing operational approaches to addressing indigenous peoples' matters in Bank operations, policy considerations and operational approaches outlined in this paper will be adopted as the principal thrust of the Bank's policy on indigenous peoples. Application of the policy would be within the context of country-level legal frameworks and other relevant circumstances.

Appendix

Key elements in an Indigenous Peoples Development Plan

1. As reflected in para. 38 of the policy document on indigenous peoples, responsibility for preparation of an indigenous peoples' plan rests with the relevant government or other project sponsor. The Bank will support the efforts of the government or project sponsor as necessary and appropriate. Key elements in ensuring that an appropriate indigenous peoples development plan is prepared include:
   - (i) preparation, during project design, of a development plan that takes into full account the desires and preferred options of indigenous peoples affected by the project;
   - (ii) studies to identify potential adverse effects on indigenous peoples to be induced by the project, and to identify measures to avoid, mitigate, or compensate for these adverse effects;
   - (iii) measures to ensure the capacity or the strengthening of the social, legal, and technical skills of government institutions to be responsible under the project for dealing with indigenous peoples;

(iv) involvement of appropriate existing institutions, local organisations, and non-government organisations with expertise in matters relating to indigenous peoples;

(v) consideration in project design of local patterns of social organisation, cultural belief, and ancestral territory and resource use;

(vi) support for viable and sustainable production systems that are adapted to the needs and local environments and circumstances of indigenous peoples;

(vii) avoidance of creating or aggravating the dependency of indigenous peoples on project entities, and instead promoting self-reliance among these peoples;

(viii) capacity building for indigenous peoples communities and organisations to facilitate and support effective participation in development processes; and

(ix) adequate lead time and arrangements for extending follow-up, especially in dealing with indigenous peoples in remote or neglected areas where little previous experience is available. Consultation with indigenous peoples groups is key to developing an effective, accurate, responsive indigenous peoples development plan.

2. Indigenous peoples often lack the information, knowledge, analytical and organisational capacities, and political channels and power to influence and direct development processes that directly or indirectly affect their lives. The following basic principles should apply to Bank-supported projects that affect indigenous peoples:

(i) All development plans for indigenous peoples, including provisions for mitigation measures, should be based on full consideration of the options and approaches, including requirements for consultation, that best meet the interests of individuals and communities affected by projects. Qualified specialists should be involved in the formulation of such plans and mitigation measures, in consultation with the persons affected, both men and women. The development of approaches, plans, and mitigation measures must include consultation with the peoples' affected.

(ii) When it is indicated that a project will have adverse effects on indigenous peoples, it is necessary that the scope and impact of such adverse effects be thoroughly assessed by qualified experts or agencies, and that appropriate mitigation measures are identified in feasibility studies. It is preferable that the net impact a project will have on indigenous peoples not only be positive, but also be perceived by indigenous peoples as positive. If individuals or communities must lose their social support systems or ways of life so that a project can proceed, they should be compensated appropriately.

(iii) Project design should take into consideration the social and cultural context of affected peoples, and their skills and knowledge relating to local resource management. Project design should draw upon the strengths of indigenous peoples organisations and communities, as well as traditional social organisations and indigenous knowledge, and as far as feasible should avoid introducing undesirable or unacceptable changes in the way of life of indigenous communities.

(iv) During project preparation, those preparing the project should promote the formation or strengthening of indigenous peoples' organisations to facilitate their participation in project identification, planning, execution, and evaluation. As needed, provision should be made to train indigenous peoples in project management activities.

(v) Where previous experience and knowledge of working successfully with indigenous peoples is lacking, pilot-scale operations should be carried out and evaluated prior to the execution of full-scale efforts.

(vi) If government institutions responsible for interaction with indigenous peoples do not possess the necessary legal, social, and technical capacities, or if their relationship with indigenous peoples is weak, the involvement of experienced local community organisations and nongovernment organisations that can serve as intermediaries and that are acceptable to all parties involved, including governments, should be sought. Consideration should be given to traditional representative institutions. Approaches to developing the capacity of government institutions should be explored.

(vii) Bank approval of a project should not be based only on the concept and quality of project design, but also on the orientation, capacity, and operational record of the government agencies or other project sponsors concerned in executing the project.

Notes

1. "Indigenous peoples" as used in this paper encompasses a generic concept not easily reflected in a single term. Other terms relating to the concept of indigenous peoples as addressed in this working paper include "cultural minorities", "ethnic minorities", "indigenous cultural communities", "tribals," "scheduled tribes", "natives", and "aboriginals". Accepted or preferred terms and definitions vary country by country, by academic discipline, and even by the usage of groups concerned. "Indigenous peoples" is the term used in United Nations documents, and is used throughout this paper solely for convenience.
2. For a detailed explanation of the ISA, see *Guidelines for Incorporation of Social Dimensions in Bank Operations*, Asian Development Bank, Manila, October 1993, pp. 23-26. For specific approaches to the ISA, including sectoral checklists of relevant concerns, see *Handbook for Incorporation of Social Dimensions In Projects,* Asian Development Bank, Manila, May 1994.
3. Memorandum "Staff Instructions on Certain Policy/ Administrative Issues," 15 February 1994.

Part IV
Other Initiatives

Introduction

The last part of this compilation has two documents. The first deals with a document prepared by the Commonwealth Policy Studies Unit which presented this document to the Common Wealth regarding the issues of the indigenous peoples. The Commonwealth Policy Studies Unit (CPSU) is the think-tank for the Commonwealth of fifty-four nations and nearly two billion citizens. It specialises on issues of Commonwealth policy including globalisation, democracy, civil society and human rights.

There are two compelling reasons why the Commonwealth Policy Studies Unit prepared this document. It is a fact that there are 20 Commonwealth countries in which Indigenous issues seem particularly important. These are: Bangladesh, India, Pakistan and Sri Lanka (South Asia); Botswana, Cameroon, Kenya, Namibia, Nigeria, South Africa, Tanzania and Uganda (Africa); Australia, Fiji, Malaysia, New Zealand, and Papua New Guinea (Pacific and Southeast Asia); and Belize, Canada and Guyana (Caribbean and Americas). Secondly, 'The Commonwealth must recognise and address the rights of its indigenous peoples. It is no longer acceptable to dismiss indigenous issues as the domain of nation states. The Commonwealth is lagging behind other international fora and needs to bring itself up to date on this issue'.

Interestingly, the Indigenous Rights in the Commonwealth, The Australian Report also acknowledges the fact that the Commonwealth's failure to initiate special programs for its indigenous citizens can no longer be ignored. For over fifty years now the Commonwealth has developed a very positive role in promoting an educational and social agenda to benefit millions of people around the world. Yet, the needs of a substantial number of citizens have been deliberately avoided as the Commonwealth insists that indigenous policy is best left to nation states and the United Nations.

The Memorandum argues that many Commonwealth countries have not treated their Indigenous peoples fairly or justly. The Commonwealth association and some of its member states have been negligent in giving Indigenous rights the attention they deserve. This is irrespective of the fact that in the Harare Commonwealth Declaration (1991), Governments committed themselves to take action to promote the human rights of their citizens and this includes the human rights of Indigenous peoples. It is time that the Commonwealth countries make amendments and address the issues of the indigenous peoples.

The second selection in this part deals with the Indigenous Peoples' Support Organisations. Some of these are UN related and some are by the indigenous peoples themselves and are by the friends of indigenous peoples. We are presenting here only a sample of the support organisations to give an idea of the large number of initiatives to address the issues of the indigenous peoples.

18

Recognising and Protecting Indigenous Peoples' Rights in the Commonwealth

Commonwealth Policy Studies Unit Memorandum to the Commonwealth Heads of Government attending CHOGM, Coolum, Australia, 2-5 March 2002

1. This Memorandum is based on the research undertaken by the Indigenous Rights in the Commonwealth Project, a three year research and advocacy programme, based at the Commonwealth Policy Studies Unit (CPSU), during its first year of work, 2001/2.

2. The overall aim of the project is to shed light on the human rights situation of Indigenous groups, and to persuade the Commonwealth association — governments and non-governmental bodies — to give priority to its improvement. For reasons of practicality the project is focusing on 20 Commonwealth countries in which Indigenous issues seem particularly important. These are: Bangladesh, India, Pakistan and Sri Lanka (South Asia); Botswana, Cameroon, Kenya, Namibia, Nigeria, South Africa, Tanzania and Uganda (Africa); Australia, Fiji, Malaysia, New Zealand, and Papua New Guinea (Pacific and Southeast Asia); and Belize, Canada and Guyana (Caribbean and Americas).

3. This Memorandum calls on the Heads of Government meeting in Coolum, to include support for Indigenous rights in the forthcoming Commonwealth Declaration.
4. Research done during the initial stage of the project has revealed that the Commonwealth of Nations can and should do more to protect and promote Indigenous rights.
5. Commonwealth countries have a special interest in recognising and protecting the rights of Indigenous peoples, of whom approximately 150 million live in the 54 member states.
6. This is unfinished business for an association built on the national independence which replaced an empire. Indigenous peoples in these new states are today frequently disempowered and subjected to discrimination with regard to jobs, education, welfare, culture, and language, especially in relation to their land rights.
7. Many Commonwealth countries have not treated their Indigenous peoples fairly or justly. The Commonwealth association and some of its member states have been negligent in giving Indigenous rights the attention they deserve. It is time that the Commonwealth made amends.
8. This is important because in the Harare Commonwealth Declaration (1991), Governments committed themselves to take action to promote the human rights of their citizens and this includes the human rights of Indigenous peoples.
9. Commonwealth human rights policy must recognise the special situation of Indigenous peoples. It must recognise their marginalisation, their vulnerability, their lack of development, and the legitimacy of their goals of distinct group survival.
10. Initial project research suggests that Indigenous peoples, and the realisation of their economic, social and cultural rights, are a particular concern to the Commonwealth nation states, if the international development targets (IDTs), which were endorsed by Commonwealth leaders at their Edinburgh summit in 1997, are to be reached.
11. The issue of Indigenous rights has been placed firmly on

the agenda of other international organisations, such as the United Nations and the European Union, as part of their commitment to the protection and promotion of human rights.

12. The Commonwealth of nations is lagging behind current international efforts to acknowledge and protect the rights of Indigenous communities.
13. Commonwealth nations are urged to support international efforts to promote and protect Indigenous peoples' rights, such as; the United Nations draft Declaration on the Rights of Indigenous Peoples, and to conclude their negotiations on the draft Declaration before 2004,[1] and adopt the draft Declaration as it is currently formulated and; the Declaration and Plan of Action from the United Nations World Conference against Racism, Durban, South Africa, September 2001, in so far as it is consistent with the draft UN Declaration on the Rights of Indigenous Peoples.
14. In the absence of a consensus or policy as such on the issue of Indigenous peoples, it is left to each Commonwealth government to deal with Indigenous people's issues in the context of their national policies.
15. Today, however, Indigenous peoples' human rights are routinely flouted around the Commonwealth and many member states' policies are not consistent with the Commonwealth's fundamental political values, nor with the emerging norms and standards being set at the international level.
16. While there are cases of good practice among the fifty-four states which give much scope for active precedent; in 1999, Canada granted one of its Indigenous communities the right of self-determination when it returned one-fifth of the country to the political control of the Inuit, bringing into being a new and unconventional political entity called Nunavut, during the past year alone, the situation of a number of Indigenous communities in Commonwealth countries has deteriorated rapidly.

17. The Basarwa (San Bushmen) of the Kalahari Desert in Botswana today face a bleak future in relocation camps as the Government forces the remaining 700 members of their tribal group off the land where their ancestors hunted more than 20,000 years ago, in the name of wildlife conservation and 'development'.
18. The Ogiek people of Kenya are currently facing eviction by the Government from the Mau mountain forest where they have lived since time immemorial, in order to open up the area for logging companies, in contravention of Kenya's Forest Act, and in defiance of international opinion and the Ogiek's rights under international law, endangering not only the survival of the Ogiek as a people, but also the environment.
19. In Belize, the Maya people are today struggling to preserve their land rights and to protect the rainforest from the depredations of logging companies.
20. Many Amerindian communities in Guyana have not had their land titles recognised and large tracts are being handed out in timber concessions.
21. In Malaysia, the Orang Asli are today struggling for control over their traditional territories and resources.
22. In India, the survival of the Jarawa of the Andaman Islands is under threat, and Adivasis across the country often suffer gross violations of their rights.
23. In Bangladesh, the Jumma people face continuing human rights violations by the security forces and Bengali settlers in the Chittagong Hill Tracts.
24. In New Zealand, the Maori continue to suffer from poverty and landlessness in their long wait for the Treaty of Waitangi to be honoured.
25. In Australia, despite the Native Title Act, 1993, only a handful of native title claims have since been recognised.
26. Unlike the official Commonwealth, the Commonwealth Non-Governmental bodies, have seen the Commonwealth as having a special potential for assisting Indigenous peoples to realise their rights.

27. In 'Put Our World to Rights' (1991), the Commonwealth Human Rights Initiative (CHRI) made protection of Indigenous rights one of its eight human rights priorities for the Commonwealth. It recommended that: *'Commonwealth human rights policy must recognise the special situation of Indigenous and tribal peoples. It must recognise their marginalisation, their vulnerability and the legitimacy of their goals of distinct group survival'.*

28. In its Millennium Report, 'Human Rights and Poverty Eradication – A Talisman for the Commonwealth', 2001, the CHRI reiterated its plea to Commonwealth member states to recognise and protect Indigenous rights. It comments: *'Wherever they live...indigenous peoples encounter discrimination, intolerance and prejudice. They must struggle for both their survival and their identity'.*

29. Paragraph 12 of the Commonwealth People's Communiqué, October 2001, refers directly to the need for the Commonwealth nations to recognise and address the rights of Indigenous peoples:

    'The Commonwealth must recognise and address the rights of its indigenous peoples. It is no longer acceptable to dismiss indigenous issues as the domain of nation states. The Commonwealth is lagging behind other international fora and needs to bring itself up to date on this issue'.

30. Despite the continued absence of a consensus or policy on Indigenous rights, there have recently been some welcome developments by the official Commonwealth in the field of Indigenous rights.

31. The Commonwealth Foundation, an intergovernmental organisation with a mandate from Commonwealth Heads of Government, is increasingly acknowledging that Commonwealth member states need to listen to the voices and needs of Indigenous peoples if they are to fulfill their obligation to strengthening civil society and good governance.[2]

32. However, it is disappointing that in many of the reports

undertaken for the Commonwealth Foundation 'Citizens and Governance: Civil Society in the New Millennium' programme, Indigenous peoples are not acknowledged.

33. In a recent publication by the Commonwealth Secretariat, 'National Human Rights Institutions (NHRI): Best Practice', 2001, the Secretariat recognised that it needed to 'work to prevent their [Indigenous peoples'] social, political and economic marginalisation'.[3]

34. However, as this publication demonstrates, the official Commonwealth remains reluctant to acknowledge the collective rights of Indigenous peoples, despite the increasing support that the concept is receiving by UN member states at the inter-sessional Working Group on the draft UN Declaration.[4] As such, many of the needs of Indigenous peoples living within Commonwealth member states cannot be adequately addressed.

35. The CPSU calls on the Commonwealth of nations to obtain a consensus or policy on the issue of Indigenous peoples, as part of its commitment to the promotion and protection of human rights. The research undertaken by the project reveals that it cannot be left to each Commonwealth government to deal with Indigenous people's issues in the context of their national policies.

Recommendations to CHOGM:[5]

This Memorandum outlines the specific recommendations emerging from Indigenous consultations coordinated by the CPSU as part of the project, for the Commonwealth Heads of Government Meeting. The Unit seeks to encourage Commonwealth member states to:

- Recognise that Indigenous peoples have rights that need to be protected and that Indigenous rights must be an integral part of any serious programme for the realisation of human rights;
- Recognise Indigenous peoples as 'peoples' with the right to freely determine their own future themselves, a future free from discrimination on the basis of race and one where all peoples are equal. In this context, they should

support the right of all peoples, including Indigenous peoples to self-determination;

- Acknowledge and take responsibility for the colonisation process and its impact on Indigenous peoples;
- Accept responsibility to take specific action to recognise and respect Indigenous peoples' rights and to have this reflected in the forthcoming Commonwealth Declaration; such as:
  - Establishing an Indigenous Advocacy Unit within the Commonwealth Secretariat, to channel specific enquiry, advocacy or support;
  - Establishing an Expert Working Group on Indigenous Peoples to report to future CHOGMs on current needs and possible future action;
  - Inaugurating a High Commissioner for Human Rights, who would take up the issue of Indigenous peoples' rights in the Commonwealth;
- **A commitment to review national and international policies that adversely affect the rights of Indigenous peoples, such as:**
- Recognising the need to protect Indigenous peoples' land ownership rights;
- Noting the requirements of existing international standards, particularly the ICERD General Recommendation XX111 and ILO Convention No. 169, that free, prior and informed consent of Indigenous peoples be obtained in all matters of development that affect them;
- Supporting the principle that states and intergovernmental organisations, such as the Commonwealth, the World Bank, the IMF, regional banks, and the WTO, should together with Indigenous peoples review the impacts of their laws, policies and programmes with the goal of revising those that are incompatible with protection of the rights of Indigenous peoples, including the right to development;

- Supporting the principle that states provide effective remedies, recourses, redress and other measures for the loss and destruction of Indigenous lands, natural resources, and environment, resulting from exploration and exploitation and extractive activities and programmes;
- **Support policies that assist Indigenous advancement, such as:**
- Supporting a reference in the forthcoming Commonwealth Declaration calling on Commonwealth Governments to conclude their negotiations on the draft UN Declaration on the Rights of Indigenous Peoples before 2004 and adopt the Declaration as it is currently drafted;
- Effectively implementing, with the necessary funding and personnel, the UN Permanent Forum on Indigenous Issues;
- Incorporating the Declaration and Plan of Action from the United Nations World Conference against Racism, Durban, South Africa, September 2001, into the forthcoming Commonwealth Declaration, as they apply to Indigenous peoples, and in so far as they are consistent with the draft UN Declaration on the Rights of Indigenous Peoples.

It is important that this CHOGM breaks new ground with regard to Indigenous rights and that the forthcoming Commonwealth Declaration acknowledges the need to protect the rights of Indigenous peoples, and that Commonwealth leaders follow up with further commitments.

Notes

1. The year 2004 marks the close of the International Decade of the World's Indigenous Peoples (1995-2004).
2. As part of its 'Citizens and Governance: Civil Society in the New Millennium' programme, the Commonwealth Foundation published a report on Indigenous peoples (Maori) in New Zealand, April 1999.

3. See 'Indigenous Peoples' Section 6.6 in Chapter 6, 'Significant Issues' in 'National Human Rights Institutions (NHRI): Best Practice', 2001.
4. At the fifty-eighth session of the inter-sessional Working Group on the draft UN Declaration on the Rights of Indigenous Peoples, 27 January-8 February 2002, many UN member states accepted the collective rights of Indigenous peoples.
5. These recommendations were endorsed at the Dialogue on Indigenous Rights in the Commonwealth, held at Emmanuel College, University of Queensland, on October 3rd, 2001, organised by the Commonwealth Policy Studies Unit (CPSU), in association with the University of Queensland; at the Forum of Indigenous Peoples in the Commonwealth, held at Brisbane City Hall, on 4 October 2001, sponsored by the Commonwealth Association of Indigenous Peoples (CAIP), and at the South Pacific Regional Expert Meeting on Indigenous Rights in the Commonwealth, held in Nadi, Fiji Islands, on 15-16 October 2001, organised by the CPSU.

19

Indigenous Peoples' Support Organisations

2.1 International Working Group for Indigenous Affairs (IWGIA)

IWGIA is an international human rights organisation which supports indigenous peoples around the world. IWGIA's overall goal is to endorse and promote indigenous peoples' right to self-determination, their cultural integrity and their right to development on their own conditions. In order to fulfil this task, IWGIA works within a wide range of areas: Documentation, publication, human rights, lobbying, advocacy, research and projects.

IWGIA is an independent international membership organisation staffed by specialists and advisers on indigenous affairs. The **aims and activities of** IWGIA are: it supports indigenous peoples' struggle for human rights, self-determination, right to territory, control of land and resources, cultural integrity, and the right to development.

- IWGIA collaborates with indigenous peoples' organisations all over the world.
- Documentation about indigenous affairs is an essential part of IWGIA's work. IWGIA publishes books, periodicals and a yearbook about indigenous peoples.
- IWGIA holds consultative status with the United Nations Economic and Social Council (ECOSOC) and is an observer to the Arctic Council.

- The basis for IWGIA's activities is an integrated approach which aims to combine the key activities documentation and publication, human rights work, political lobbying and projects. IWGIA's work is primarily funded by the Nordic Ministries of Foreign Affairs and the European Union.

IWGIA's work with indigenous peoples is, first of all, guided by a rights based approach. A key principle for IWGIA is that human rights are a fundamental tool for improving the economic and political situation of marginalised indigenous peoples. Indigenous peoples are in many cases excluded from decision-making processes concerning their future. They are often deprived of their basic human rights, and examples of discrimination are numerous. A basic principle for IWGIA is that indigenous peoples' rights should be recognised and respected by the state in which the peoples live, and by the society that surrounds them, and that indigenous peoples should be involved in all decisions that concern their future.

IWGIA works with all the human rights regimes including political, economic, social and cultural rights. We put special emphasis on collective rights such as the right to self-determination and development on their own conditions, indigenous peoples' collective rights to land, the right to non-discrimination and the right to retain their own language and culture.

A key principle for IWGIA's work is the promotion of the right to self-determination. Self-determination embodies the right for all peoples to determine their own economic, social and cultural development. Self-determination implies the right to participate in the democratic process of governance and decision-making and for indigenous peoples to determine their own future. It is important to stress that for most indigenous peoples the term self-determination does not imply secession from the state.

Indigenous women experience many forms of discrimination, not only from the surrounding society but also from within their own communities. In situations of armed conflict they are also particular targets of violence and oppression. Although women play a crucial role both as reproducers, producers and caretakers of their societies and cultures, and of the well being of their communities, the importance of their social role is not always recognised. In many places indigenous women are increasingly becoming aware and critical of their status and the ways in which they are treated, and they try to organise themselves and assert their rights as women and as indigenous people. IWGIA wishes to promote gender relations based on equity and mutual respect.

2.2 The International Alliance of Indigenous and Tribal Peoples of the Tropical Forests – IAITPTF

The International Alliance of Indigenous and Tribal Peoples of the Tropical Forests is a worldwide network of organisations representing indigenous and tribal peoples living in tropical forest regions (Africa, the Asia-Pacific and the Americas). The Alliance was founded in 1992 during an indigenous conference in Malaysia, where the Charter of the Alliance was adopted, and has been fighting continuously for the rights of indigenous

The objectives of the Alliance are to:

- promote full recognition of the rights and territories of indigenous and tribal peoples;
- promote the development of indigenous and tribal peoples and their participation in decision and policy making;
- establish effective networks between indigenous peoples at regional and international levels;
- exchange information and experiences to empower Alliance members to advocate for the rights of indigenous and tribal peoples, enabling them to impact upon processes falling within the complex UN system, and the policies and decision-making of developmental agencies and multi-lateral development banks;
- promote worldwide solidarity between indigenous and tribal peoples.

The Alliance is coordinated by an International Coordinating Committee (ICC), which meets at least twice a year to monitor the work of the Alliance. The Committee is constituted of 9 Regional Coordinators. Supported by a regional secretariat and the International Technical Secretariat, each Regional Coordinator represents one of the nine regions falling within the Alliance's remit. Any indigenous-led organisation based in a tropical forest country can become a member of the Alliance.

2.3. Working Group on Indigenous Populations (OHCHR)

Following a reform to the UN human Rights machinery, the Human Rights Council adopted resolution 6/16 to request the Office of the High Commissioner for Human Rights to convene an informal meeting to discuss the most appropriate mechanisms to continue the work of the working Group on Indigenous Populations. The Informal meeting took place in Geneva on 6 December and the morning of 7 December 2007.

As a follow-up to the informal meeting the indigenous caucus and a number of governments continued informal negotiations to finalise a draft resolution and submitted to the resumed 6th session of the Human Rights Council. On December 14, 2007 draft resolution A/HRC/6/L.42 (HRC Resolution 6/36) establishing a new expert mechanism on the rights of indigenous peoples was adopted by consensus by the HRC.

The Human Rights Council decided to establish an Expert Body on the Rights of Indigenous Peoples:

(a) to provide the Council with expert advice on Indigenous Peoples' and individuals' human rights in relation to all the Council's mandates;

(b) to identify and recommend to the Council effective mechanisms to implement, develop and mainstream international standards that promote and protect the human rights of Indigenous Peoples;

(c) to review, elaborate and follow-up on best practices as well as obstacles for the promotion and protection of Indigenous Peoples' human rights;

(d) to review and undertake studies and focused research on human rights issues as they relate to Indigenous Peoples. States, Indigenous Peoples and their representative institutions will be invited to present statements, case studies and papers on situations pertaining to the realisation of the rights of Indigenous Peoples;

(e) to cooperate, with a view to complement their respective work, with other relevant mechanisms on the rights of Indigenous Peoples, including the Permanent Forum on Indigenous Issues, the Special Rapporteur on the situation of human rights and fundamental freedoms of Indigenous people and other relevant special procedures, the Human Rights Council Advisory Committee, the Treaty Bodies, the Office of the High Commissioner for Human Rights, and regional, national and Indigenous Peoples' human rights institutions;

(f) to perform other tasks at the request of the Council.

It was also decided that the Expert Body should be placed directly under the Human Rights Council and report annually to this Council on its work.

2.4 Indigenous Peoples' Issues and Resources

Indigenous Peoples' Issues and Resources is a worldwide network of organisations, academics, activists, indigenous groups, and others representing indigenous and tribal peoples. It consists of a concerned group of social scientists, activists, scholars, laypeople, indigenous people, and others who all share a combined goal: to provide resources, news, articles, and information on current issues affecting indigenous and tribal peoples around the world. Founded in 2007 by Peter N. Jones, *Indigenous Peoples' Issues and Resources* has quickly grown into a network of subscribers, contributors, and supporters across the globe. *Indigenous Peoples' Issues and Resources* has been fighting continuously for the rights of indigenous and tribal peoples since its inception.

The mission of the *Indigenous Peoples' Issues and Resources* is to fight for the rights of indigenous and tribal peoples. This mission is accomplished by:

- promoting full recognition of the rights and territories of indigenous and tribal peoples.
- promoting the development of indigenous and tribal peoples and their participation in decision and policy making.
- establishing effective networks between indigenous and tribal peoples at regional, state, and international levels

- exchanging information and experiences to empower members to advocate for the rights of indigenous and tribal peoples, enabling them to have a positive impact
- to provide articles, videos, resources, news, and information concerning indigenous and tribal peoples
- promoting worldwide solidarity between indigenous and tribal peoples.

2.5 The Asian Indigenous Women's Network (AIWN)

The first Asian Indigenous Women's Conference was held in Baguio City in the Cordillera region, Philippines on January 24-30, 1993. The conference brought together 150 women from 13 Asian countries and a few others from Europe and the Americas with the bulk of the participants coming from local organisations in the Cordillera. Its theme was 'Sharing Commonalities and Diversities, Forging Unity Towards Indigenous Women's Empowerment.' Its general objective was 'to convene Asian indigenous women to share their various situations, fully understand how global developments impact on them, and collectively define what they can do to address common concerns.' The conference gave birth to the Asian Indigenous Women's Network (AIWN), which the participants then envisioned as a loose network that would help organise indigenous women in the region. The Cordillera Women's Education and Resource Center (CWERC) was the key organiser of the conference.

On March 4-8, 2004, AIWN held its 2nd Asian Indigenous Women's Conference with the theme: 'Heightening Empowerment and Solidarity of Indigenous Women in Asia.' The successful conference was attended by 108 participants from 37 indigenous peoples' organisations (11 indigenous women's organisations and 26 indigenous peoples' organisations with women committees) and 32 support organisations (non-government, academe and government agencies) from 13 Asian countries. The conference resulted to the Baguio Declaration of the Second Asian Indigenous Women's Conference which outlines indigenous women's concerns/ issues and recommendations.

2.6 Aliansi Masyarakat Adat Nusantara (AMAN)

AMAN or Indigenous Peoples Alliance of the Archipelago is an independent social organisation composed of indigenous peoples' communities from the whole of the country. The Alliance is aimed to be an organisation for indigenous peoples to struggle for their existence and rights inherited with it as well as to struggle for sovereignty in running their lives and in managing their natural resources.

AMAN was founded in 1999 and at the time of its third Congress in 2007, the number of Indigenous communities that had registered to become AMAN members totaled 1016. From this number, a total of 695 indigenous communities are verified members.

The programmes of AMAN are:

- to work on the efforts to establish, to develop, and to strengthen indigenous organisations throughout Indonesia as community-based organisations with an effective information and communication center.
- to accelerate the change of political sphere at national level to go up to democratic political lives where legal systems are able to guarantee and to protect indigenous peoples rights.
- to raise the bargaining power of production and distribution system of indigenous peoples' economic resources to defend their system from the intervention of new exploitative economic system leading to over dependency and consumerism.
- to raise political and gender awareness among indigenous women and to initiate and to facilitate indigenous women organisation development at local, regional, and national level.
- to bridge the gap in indigenous knowledge and wisdom between old and young generation of an indigenous community and to build strong indigenous cultural identity and character among indigenous youth in terms of diversity and pluralism.

2.7 Tebtebba (Indigenous Peoples' International Centre for Policy Research and Education)

Tebtebba is an indigenous peoples' organisation born out of the need for heightened advocacy to have the rights of indigenous peoples recognised, respected and protected worldwide. Established in 1996, Tebtebba seeks to promote a better understanding of the world's indigenous peoples, their worldviews, their issues and concerns. In this effort, it strives to bring indigenous peoples together to take the lead in policy advocacy and campaigns on all issues affecting them.

Tebtebba, a word used by the indigenous Kankana-ey Igorots of Northern Philippines, refers to a process of collectively discussing issues and presenting diverse views with the aim of reaching agreements, common positions, and concerted actions.

The vision of Tebtebba world where indigenous knowledge and indigenous peoples' rights are respected and protected by all nations and societies; where there are unified yet diverse and vibrant indigenous peoples' movements at the local and global levels which enhance the self-determination and sustainable development of indigenous peoples' and their territories.

Tebtebba is an indigenous peoples' organisation and a research, education, policy advocacy and resource center working with indigenous peoples at all levels and arenas. We seek the recognition, promotion and protection of indigenous peoples' rights and aspirations while building unities to uphold social and environmental justice and sustainability. We shall achieve this by reinforcing the capacities of indigenous peoples for advocacy, campaigns and networking; research, education, training, and institutional development, and by actively articulating and projecting indigenous peoples' views and perspectives.

2.8 International Indian Treaty Council – IITC

The IITC was founded in 1974 at a gathering by the American Indian Movement in Standing Rock, South Dakota attended by more than 5,000 representatives of 98 Indigenous Nations. When IITC was established, the following were the objectives:

- Implementation of an effective plan of action for the International Decade of the World's Indigenous Peoples which began on December 10th, 1994.
- Adoption of the Draft Declaration for the Rights of Indigenous Peoples.
- Development of a permanent forum for Indigenous Peoples within the UN system.

Along with this, IITC also addressed violations of Indigenous Peoples' rights and presenting issues of concern to the international community. Primary focus areas include:

- Protection and Sustainable Development. Treaty and Land Rights.
- Cultural Rights, Sacred sites and Religious Freedom.
- Rights and protection of Indigenous Children.

In 1977, the IITC became the first organisation of Indigenous Peoples to be reorganised as a NGO with Consultative Status to the United Nations Economic and Social Council. The IITC focuses on building Indigenous Peoples' participation in key UN fora such as the Commission on Human Rights, the Working Group on Indigenous Populations, the Sub-Commission on Prevention of Discrimination and Protection of Minorities, the Conference of the Parties to the Convention on Biological Diversity, UNESCO and the Commission on Sustainable Development. In recent years, IITC has also participated in the International Labor Organisation (ILO), UN World Conferences, the International Union for the Conservation of Nature (IUCN) and the World Archeological Congress to systematically address concerns vital to Indigenous Peoples.

IITC continues to submit and monitor human rights complaints filed on behalf of Indigenous Peoples facing violations of their freedom of religion, forced relocations, arbitrary detentions and other crisis situations.

2.9 Indigenous Peoples' Global Research and Education Network (IPGREN)

Indigenous peoples are increasingly becoming weary and wary of researches that only treat them as targets of research and education efforts. In the area of research, indigenous peoples have always been the sources of information. Much of these information, when processed and interpreted by the researchers, become unintelligible if not totally irrelevant to the indigenous peoples' everyday lives. Indigenous Peoples want to speak out now. They want to conduct research that can help them articulate their issues and perspectives. They want to (re)claim an arena where they have been historically marginalised. At the same time, they want to be trained on the rudiments of 'scientific inquiry,' if only to better understand their changing social, cultural and environmental milieu and become more effective in putting forward their issues and concerns.

The IPGREN is envisaged to be the machinery that is to carry out the indigenous peoples research and education agenda. The IPGREN was envisioned to be a network of individuals, organisations and institutions (NGOs, academic research institutes, etc.) who are committed to a Participatory Action Research (PAR), on issues and concerns affecting indigenous peoples. The network is organised and managed by an international coordinating committee with the assistance of Tebtebba as the secretariat.

All the indigenous peoples' organisations and individuals present at the December 2000 conference in Manila have signified interest to become members of this network. However, other organisations and individuals are also free to join. While IPGREN is aimed to be an international forum, there will be regional focal points (individuals and/or institutions) for Asia, Latin America, Africa and the Pacific Regions.

2.10 International Indigenous Women's Forum/Foro Internacional de Mujeres Indígenas (IIWF/FIMI)

FIMI was established in 1995 during the Fourth World Conference on Women (also known as the Beijing Conference, named after its host city). Given that more than 30 thousand women attended, it was one of the largest UN conferences ever held. The indigenous women's organisations were some of the most active and effective participants at the Beijing Conference. As a result of their participation, they have been able to create and strengthen international networks of indigenous activists, develop leadership abilities and make the concerns of indigenous communities known on an international level. As a result of their work, the Platform for Action directly addressed the role of indigenous women.

Five years later many of the Beijing participants returned for the follow-up meeting, known as Beijing+5. This time, before everyone returned to their homes in different parts of the world, the indigenous women decided to create an organisation that could continue with the international organising, promotion and advocacy work that began during the conference. The result was the International Indigenous Women's Forum, or FIMI.

FIMI's mission is to bring together indigenous women activists, leaders and human rights promoters from different parts of the world for the purpose of coordinating agendas, building unity, developing leadership and advocacy skills, increasing indigenous women's participation in international decision-making procedures, and advancing women's rights.

FIMI envisions a world free from all forms of discrimination, where indigenous communities can exercise their human rights, have access to economic justice, and where they can participate fully and effectively in decision-making procedures that affect their lives on a local, national, regional and international level. FIMI sees a world where all women can enjoy their fundamental human rights, one that strives to establish a new paradigm that is defined by freedom from racism, social exclusion and inequality.

2.11 Indigenous Information Network (IIN)

It is a non-profit, NGO registered in the Republic of Kenya under the Non Governmental Organisation Act of 1990. It was founded in 1996, and was legally registered in 2001. The organisation was founded by a group of professionals in response to addressing needs particularly regarding availing information through media and other channels about Indigenous Peoples, their livelihood and challenges they face as they struggle to exist. The organisation has been managed by volunteers since 1996, and has been involved in dissemination of information, environmental conservation activities, community development, and advocacy activities in support of Indigenous and Minority Peoples in the region.

The members are mainly drawn from individuals, Community Based Organisations (CBOs) and Non Governmental Organisations (NGOs) with interest in advancement of indigenous and minority peoples interests

The underlying issue that motivated the founder members of IIN is that Indigenous and Minority Peoples have been marginalised from mainstream development agenda particularly due to their ways of life (nomadic pastoralists and hunters and gatherers). IIN recognises that the way Indigenous Peoples live is sustainable and worth supporting. This belief has been supported by the organisation through the activities it has undertaken since its initiation. The organisation's main thrust is the creation of awareness of the status quo of Indigenous groups and initiation of activities that address bottlenecks hindering advancement of the systems in place.

2.12 Asian Indigenous and Tribal Peoples Network (AITPN)

The AITPN is an alliance of indigenous and tribal peoples' organisations and individual activists across the Asian region. It is based in New Delhi but works in entire Asia. It seeks to promote and protect the rights of indigenous and tribal peoples in Asia:

- by providing accurate and timely information to national human rights institutions, the United Nations and its specialised mechanisms, as appropriate;
- by conducting research, campaigning and lobbying on country situations or individual cases;
- by increasing the capacity of indigenous peoples through relevant training programmes for indigenous peoples' rights activists and community leaders;
- by providing legal, political and practical advice to indigenous peoples organisations;
- by providing input into international standard-setting processes on the rights of indigenous peoples; and

- by securing the economic, social and cultural rights of indigenous peoples through rights-based approaches to development.

AITPN has been in the forefront of making Asian indigenous peoples' submissions for inclusion into the stakeholders' summary prepared by the OHCHR. AITPN in association with a number of indigenous organisations made the stakeholders' submission on Malaysia and Bangladesh, which was examined at the fourth session of the Working Group on the Universal Periodic Review of the UN Human Rights Council (2 - 13 February 2009). AITPN has Special Consultative Status with the United Nations Economic and Social Council (ECOSOC).

AITPN also undertakes research and publication. Its recent publication is "The State of India's Indigenous and Tribal Peoples 2009". The report covers wide range of issues such as violations of the rights of the indigenous peoples by the security forces and the non-tribals, indigenous peoples and armed conflict, violations of the international humanitarian law by the armed opposition groups, violence against indigenous women and children, alienation of indigenous peoples' land, displacement of indigenous/tribal peoples, repression under forest laws, failure of affirmative action programmes and state of the National Commission for Scheduled Tribes, among others. As the editorial of this report shows, the National Human Rights Institutions, despite their various shortcomings, can be effective if effective interventions from the civil society organisations or individuals are made.

Selected Bibliography

African Commission on Human and Peoples Rights. Reports of the African Commission's Working Group on Indigenous Populations/Communities in Africa. IWGIA Document Series. 2008.

AITPN. The State of India's Indigenous and Tribal Peoples 2009. AITPN: New Delhi. 2009.

Albert Kwokwo Barume. Land Rights of Indigenous Peoples in Africa. IWGIA Document Series. 2005.

Allen Buchanan. The Theory of Collective Rights in the Theory of Indigenous People's Rights. Transnational Law and Contemporary Problems 3 (1): 89-108.

_______Justice, Legitimacy and Self-Determination. Oxford University Press: Oxford. 2003.

Alexander Ewen and Chief Oren Lyons. Voice of Indigenous Peoples: Native People Address the United Nations. Clear Light Book. 1993.

Alexandra Xanthaki. Indigenous Rights and United Nations Standards: Self-Determination, Culture and Land. Cambridge University Press: Cambridge. 2007.

Asian Development Bank. Policy on Indigenous Peoples. Manila, Philippines. 1998.

Avigail Eisenberg and Jeff Spinner-Halev (ed). Minorities within Minorities: Equality, Rights and Diversity. Cambridge University Press: UK. 2005.

Barbara Bower and Barbara Rose Johnston (ed). Disappearing Peoples? Indigenous Groups and Ethnic Minorities in South and Central Asia. Left Coast Press: California. 2007.

Bartholomew Dean and Jerome Levi (eds.) At the Risk of Being Heard: Indigenous Rights, Identity and Postcolonial States. University of Michigan Press: USA. 2003.

Benjamin J. Richardson, Shin Imai, and Kent McNei (ed). Indigenous Peoples and the Law: Comparative and Critical Perspectives. Hart Publishing: Portland. 2009.

Bradley Reed Howard. Indigenous Peoples and the State: The Struggle for Native Rights. Northern Illinois University Press: Illinois. 2003.

Bruce E. Johansen. Indigenous Peoples and Environmental Issues: An Encyclopedia. Greenwood Press: Westport. 2003.

B.D. Sharma. *Globalisation:* The Tribal Encounter. Har-Anand Publications: New Delhi. 1995.

B.G. Karlsson. Contested Belonging: an Indigenous People's Struggle for Forest and Identity in Sub-Himalayan Bengal. Curzon Press: Surrey. 2000.

B.K. Roy Burman. Workshop on Tribal Development, Intentions, Realities, Challenges and Tasks Ahead. Akhil Bharatiya Adivasi Vikas Parishad: New Delhi. 1993.

David Maybury-Lewis. *I*ndigenous Peoples, Ethnic Groups, and the State. Allyn & Bacon: New Jersey. 2001.

Deepak Acharya and Anshu Shrivastava. Indigenous Herbal Medicines: Tribal Formulations and Traditional Herbal Practices. Aavishkar Publishers Distributor: Jaipur. 2008.

Dev Nathan, Govind Kelkar and Pierre Walter (ed). Globalisation and Indigenous Peoples in Asia: Changing the Local-Global Interface. Sage Publications: New Delhi. 2004.

Duncan Ivison, Paul Patton and Will Sanders (ed). Political Theory and the Rights of the Indigenous Peoples. Cambridge University Press: Cambridge. 2008.

Edward F. Fischer (ed). Indigenous Peoples, Civil Society, and the Neo-liberal State in Latin America. Berghahn Books: Oxford. 2008.

Edward L. Cleary and Timothy J. Steigenga. Resurgent Voices in Latin America: Indigenous Peoples, Political Mobilisation, and Religious Change. Rutgers University Press: New Brunswick. 2004.

Fergus MacKay. A Guide to Indigenous Peoples Rights in the Inter-American Human Rights System. IWGIA Document Series. 2002.

Habitat International Coalition. International Human Rights Standards on Post-disaster Resettlement and Rehabilitation. Books for Change: New Delhi. 2006.

Helena Whall and Meena Shivdas. Indigenous Women's Rights: Challenging Social and Gender Hierarchies. Common Wealth Secretariat: London. 2011.

Henry Minde, Mattias Ahren and Asbiorn Eide. The UN declaration of indigenous peoples: what made it possible? : The work and process beyond the final adoption. Resource Centre for the Rights of Indigenous Peoples. 2007.

Henry Minde, Svein Jentoft and Harald Gaski. Indigenous Peoples: Self-determination, Knowledge and Indigeneity. Eburon: The Netherlands. 2008.

Hulleah J. Tshinhnahjinnie and Veronica Passalacqua (ed). Our People, Our Land, Our Images: International Indigenous Photographers. The Regents of the University of California: California. 2006.

Indian Confederation of Indigenous and Tribal Peoples. Indigenous and Tribal Solidarity: ICITP 3rd General Assembly Meeting, 1997. ICITP: New Delhi. 1997.

Jakob Kronik and Dorte Verner (ed). Indigenous Peoples and Climate Change in Latin America and the Caribbean. World Bank: Washington D.C. 2010.

Jeremie Gilbert. Indigenous Peoples' Land Rights under International Law. Transnational Publishers. 2006.

John B. Henriksen. Implementation of the Right of Self-Determination of Indigenous Peoples. Indigenous Affairs. Copenhagen: International Work Group for Indigenous Affairs. 2001.

James S. Anaya. Indigenous Peoples in International Law. Oxford University Press: Oxford. 1999.

_______International Human Rights and Indigenous Peoples (Elective Series). Oxford University Press: Oxford. 2009.

James Crawford. Peoples and Populations: Indigenous Peoples and Rights. The Clarendon Press: Oxford. 1988.

Jeffrey Sissons. First People: Indigenous Cultures and Their Futures. Reaktion Books: London. 2005.

Jerry Mander and Victoria Tauli-Corpuz (ed). Paradigm War: Indigenous Peoples' Resistance to Globalisation. Sierra Club Books: San Francisco. 2006.

Jose Martinez Cobo. Study of the Problem of Discrimination against Indigenous Populations, Vol. 5. UNESCO. 1987.

Karen Engle. The Elusive Promise of Indigenous Development: Rights, Culture, Strategy. Duke University Press: Durham. 2010.

Kenneth Coates. A Global History of Indigenous Peoples: Struggles and Survival. Palgrave Macmillan: Melbourne. 2004.

K.S. Singh (ed). Antiquity to Modernity in Tribal India. Volumes I to IV. Inter-India Publishers: New Delhi. 1998.

Linda Tuhiwai Smith. Decolonising Methodologies: Research and Indigenous Peoples. Zed Books: London. 1999.

Lindsay G. Robertson. Conquest by Law: How the Discovery of America Dispossessed Indigenous Peoples of Their Lands. Oxford University Press: Oxford. 2005.

Luis Rodriguez-Pinero. Indigenous Peoples, Postcolonialism and International Law: The ILO Regime (1919-1989). Oxford University Press: Oxford. 2005.

Makere Stewart-Harawira. The New Imperial Order: Indigenous Responses. Huia Publishers: New Zeland. 2005.

Mario Blaser, Harvery A. Feit, and Glenn McRae (ed.). In the Way of Development: Indigenous Peoples, Life Projects and Globalisation. Zed Books: London. 2004.

Mario Blaser, Ravi De Costa, Deborah McGregor, and William D. Coleman (ed). Indigenous Peoples and Autonomy: Insights for a Global Age. University of British Colombia: Vancouver. 2010.

Mario Ibarra. Annotations for a Chronology of Indigenous Peoples in International Law in Water Fernandes (ed) The Indigenous Question: Search for an Identity. Indian Social Institute: New Delhi. 1993.

Martin Daunton and Rick Halpern. Empire and Others: British Encounters with Indigenous Peoples, 1600-1850. University of Pennsylvania Press: Philadelphia. 1999.

Martin Edwin Andersen. Peoples of the Earth: Ethnonationalism, Democracy and the Indigenous Challenge in "Latin" America. Lexington Books: Lanham, 2010.

Michael C. van Walt van Praag and Onno Seroo (eds.): The Implementation of the Right to Self-Determination as a Contribution to Conflict Prevention. UNESCO Division of Human Rights; Barcelona, 1999.

Ministry of Foreign Affairs, Government of Denmark. Danish Strategy for Indigenous Peoples, 1998.

Minority Rights Group (ed.). Forests and Indigenous Peoples of Asia, Report 98/4, London, 1999.

M.A. Stephenson (ed). Mabo: The Native Title Legislation: A Legislative Response to the High Court Decision. Queensland University Press: St. Lucia. 1995.

M. Bianet Castellanos. *A Return to Servitude: Maya Migration and the Tourist Trade in Cancún.* University of Minnesota Press: Minneapolis. 2010.

Nancy Grey Postero and Leon Zamosc (ed.). The Struggle for Indigenous Rights in Latin America. Sussex Academic Press: Sussex. 2004.

Noam Chomsky, Lois Meyer, and Benjamin Maldonado. New World of Indigenous Resistance. City Light Books: San Francisco. 2010.

Pamela Martin. The Globalisation of Contentious Politics: The Amazonian Indigenous Rights Movement. Routledge: 2002.

Paul Keal. European Conquest and the Rights of Indigenous Peoples: The Moral Backwardness of International Society. Cambridge University Press: Cambridge. 2003.

Prakash Louis. "Jharkhand: Marginalisation of Tribals', *Economic and Political Weekly*, 35 (47): 4087-4091. 2000.

_______Scheduled Castes and Tribes: The Reservation Debate. *Economic and Political Weekly*. Vol. XXXVIII. No. 25, June 21-27, 2003, pp. 2475-2478.

_______Governance, Reform and Development: Scheduled Tribes in India in the Era of Globalisation. In the book Globalisation, Governance, Reforms and Development in India (ed.) Kameshwar Choudhary. Sage Publications: New Delhi. 2007.

______Rights of Scheduled Tribes of India: Acts, Commissions and Recommendations. Manak Publications, New Delhi. 2008.

Ram Dayal Munda. 'Adivasi Identity: Crisis and Way out. Rising Fascism', *Update Collective*. New Delhi: Delhi Forum. N.D.

Raymond John Pierotti. Indigenous Knowledge, Ecology and Evolutionary Biology. Routledge: UK. 2010.

Robert Hitchcock and Samuel Totten. Genocide of Indigenous Peoples: Genocide: a Critical Bibliographical Review. Transaction Publication: New Jersey. 2010.

Ronald Niezen. The Origins of Indigenism: Human Rights and the Political Identity. University of California Press: California. 2003.

Sanjay Barbora. Ethnic Politics and Land Use: Genesis of Conflicts in India's Northeast. *Economic and Political Weekly*. Vol. 37. No. 13, March 30, 2002, pp. 1285-1292.

Shirley Stewart Burns, Mari-Lynn Evans, and Silas House (ed.). Coal Country Rising Up Against Mountaintop Removal Mining. Sierra Club Books: San Francisco. 2010.

Stefano Varese. Witness to Sovereignty: Essays on the Indian Movement in Latin America. International Work Group on Indigenous Affairs; Copenhagen. 2006.

Stephen Allen and Alexandra Xanthaki (ed). Reflections on the UN Declaration on the Rights of Indigenous Peoples. Hart Publishing: UK. 2010.

Svein Jentoft, Henry Minde and Ragnar Nilsen. Indigenous Peoples: Resource Management and Global Right. Eburon: The Netherlands. 2003.

Thomas D. Hall and James V. Fenelon. *Indigenous Peoples and Globalisation: Resistance and Revitalisation.* Paradigm Publishers: Boulders. 2009.

United Nations. United Nations Declaration on the Rights of Indigenous Peoples. UNPFII. http://www.un.org/esa/socdev/unpfii/documents/DRIPS_en.pdf. Retrieved on

______Frequently Asked Questions: Declaration on the Rights of Indigenous Peoples. United Nations Permanent Forum on Indigenous Issues. http://www.un.org/esa/socdev/unpfii/documents/FAQsindigenousdeclaration.pdf. Retrieved.

______Indigenous Peoples and the United Nations System. Office of the High Commissioner for Human Rights, United Nations: Geneva. http://www.unhchr.ch/html/racism/indileaflet1.doc.

______Rights of persons belonging to national or ethnic, religious and linguistic minorities, 2005. Commission on Human Rights resolution, 2005/79. http://www.ohchr.org/english/issues/minorities/docs/Minorities%202005-eng.doc

______Human rights and indigenous issues, 2005, Commission on Human Rights resolution 2005/51, 2005.

UNHCR. World Directory of Minorities and Indigenous Peoples – Philippines: Overview. UNHCR. 2007. http:// www. ohchr.org/english/issues/indigenous/docs/2005-eng.doc

______Protection of indigenous peoples in time of conflict, 2005, Commission on Human Rights resolution 2005/52, 2005. http://www.ohchr.org/english/issues/indigenous/docs/2005-eng.doc

______Working Group on Indigenous Populations of the Sub-Commission on the Promotion and Protection of Human Rights, 2005, Commission on Human Rights resolution 2005/49. http://www.ohchr.org/english/issues/indigenous/docs/2005-eng.doc

Virginus Xaxa. *The Adivasis of India.* A paper prepared for Department for International Development (DIFD). Memo. N.D.

Walter Fernandes, Gita Bharali and Vemedo Kezo (ed). *The UN Indigenous Decade in Northeast India.* Northeastern Social Research Centre: Guwahati. 2008.

Will Kymlicka and Wayne Norman (ed). Citizenship in Diverse Societies. Oxford University Press: Oxford. 2000.

Relevant Websites

http://indigenouspeoplesissues.com

http://www.un.org/esa/socdev/unpfii/en/declaration.html

http://www.un.org/esa/socdev/unpfii

www.cpsu.org.uk

www.international-alliance.org

www.un.org

http://www.treatycouncil.org/new_page_523131.htm
http://www.asianindigenouswomen.org
http://aman.or.id/
http://www.indigenouspeople.net
http://www.tebtebba.org
http://www.aaanet.org/committees/cfhr/orgindig.htm
www.aitpn.org
http://www.twnside.org.sg/title/dec-ch.htm

Index